UNSTUCKABLE

UNSTABLE

To all the ambitious
who always want something more.

UCK

Never Be Stuck
in Business Again
with Tools from
Tech Innovators

HEATHER KERNAHAN

Cataloguing in publication information is
available from Library and Archives Canada.
ISBN: 978-1-77458-418-7 (paperback)
ISBN: 978-1-77458-419-4 (ebook)

Page Two
pagetwo.com

Edited by Sarah Brohman
Copyedited by Melissa Kawaguchi
Cover and interior design by Jennifer Lum

unstuckable.me

CONTENTS

INTRODUCTION

I HAD FIVE HOURS to get to San Francisco, and the stakes
for what was coming could not be higher. As I sat on the
plane with shaky knees and sweaty palms, my racing mind
would not quit telling me all the ways I could fuck up the
next thirty-six hours.

The tech company I had dedicated years to had been
bought by our biggest competitor, and I was on my way to
meet them. As the countdown for the deal closing ticked on,
and rumors about layoffs and office shutdowns swirled around
the company, I realized that all other thoughts would have to
wait. My focus was on creating a clear vision of what I wanted
to achieve in the meetings ahead and how to convey my value
and potential to the acquiring team.

With almost a decade spent in the center of tech innovation, I had helped develop globally renowned brands and had
been part of teams that had pushed the edges to build new
technology. Immersed in a culture that thrived on continuous
learning, absorbed setbacks, and swiftly adjusted strategies,
my perspective of work and self-identity had transformed

dramatically. Life was now a matrix of opportunities and choices. Yet, as the plane cut through the clouds, carrying me to a destiny unknown, fear gripped me. Was I on the edge of a fall, or was this the start of a new era? My past successes seemed meaningless in the face of an uncertain future. My worst fear was that I would stop moving forward—a fate worse than failure for me.

Trying to get control over my chaotic thoughts, I opened my notebook and started to list what I had learned from working in the tech industry and how those techniques and lessons could help me redefine the next stage of my career, whether that was in a role with the acquiring company or going in a different direction. That list was the beginning of a framework of ideas, tools, and important questions that I could pull from to keep me unstuck with options always available. Right there, on that plane, a blueprint was born. One that's guided me through that important week, the next decade, and the rest of my life. And in the decades since that trip, I have refined that model with insight from hundreds of tech leaders and shared it with colleagues, founders, investors, and leaders around the world.

I didn't always know how to get unstuck. In my early days in tech, there were many times I stumbled, faltered, made missteps, and had near disasters. Like almost being fired from my first job in tech and all the product launches that failed. Then there was the time I pissed off a very important client just ahead of a global marketing campaign because of my inability to skillfully navigate company dynamics. The resulting fallout was a scolding from my boss's boss that was so severe it made me question my survival in the industry. These experiences and countless others taught me unforgettable lessons on my professional journey. Each misstep, each stumble served as a catalyst for my learning and evolution. Unraveling the complexities of becoming unstuckable didn't come easily, but as you'll discover in the following chapters, every setback laid the groundwork for the resilient professional I was to become. Whether you are recently feeling stuck or have felt stuck for a while, I'm going to help you fast-track your success by introducing you to the UNSTUCK model. You'll get advice and direction from a partner who has navigated themselves and organizations through the unknown using the same kinds of tools that keep the tech industry moving forward.

The tech industry works at breakneck speed. World-changing visions can span mere decades rather than centuries; new advancements get coded in two-week sprints; and the whole industry is run by visionaries with the guts, audacity, and stamina to keep going in the face of any challenge. As I worked in and alongside start-ups, fast-growth companies, and global enterprises that acted like every day was a high-stakes situation for them, I started to see the similarities in how they thought, acted, and made decisions.

Over the past five years, almost every company on the planet has come to understand how critical technology is to their business and is working on their digital transformation. As a result, they have started to adopt tech ways of thinking and working. The pandemic accelerated that process. At the same time, business leaders are feeling more stuck than ever as they navigate the changing landscape. Everything in business—hell, everything in life—feels more uncertain than ever. It's scary to be working in the unknown, as business and society continue to shift, and the economy navigates through these historic times.

So, this book is an antidote for leaders who feel stuck. Perhaps you run a business or lead a team and you aren't getting the results you want. You pride yourself on always finding a way forward. You're an achiever. You expect to win. You want to lead with purpose, energy, and direction. But lately you can't seem to find the solutions to problems as readily as you have in the past.

Let me help you learn from the tech innovators, leaders, and challengers who have created an entire industry that can't get stuck. One of the best mistakes of my life was stumbling into the technology industry. That mistake has put me in the path of teams and organizations that keep moving forward no matter how hard the challenge and ultimately go on to experience outrageous success. Leaders in tech actively seek out new ideas, inspirations, catalysts, and people to keep generating innovative solutions and finding the energy needed to keep evolving. They do this work on purpose so that they never get stuck.

With this book, I invite you to delve into my insights and tools amassed over decades spent at the center of tech and innovation. Learn from the insights and tools of tech leaders who've faced, and overcome, challenges like yours. By opening this book, you've already taken the first step toward unsticking yourself. And by the end of this book, you'll be ready to never be stuck again. You'll be unstuckable.

I recommend you read the entire book first, making notes of where you want to come back and spend more time. Then you can choose the tools to put into action immediately to get you unstuck. But first, let's look at why the phenomenon of feeling stuck is so pervasive.

1

STUCK

"Identify your problems, but give your power and energy to solutions."

TONY ROBBINS, leading coach, author, and speaker

WHEN WAS the last time you felt stuck? Six months ago? Last week? Maybe it was just this morning when you woke up early to try to work through all the challenges ahead. It can be a feeling you can't shake and haven't been able to work your way out of with your usual tools and techniques. Stuck can also be a series of thoughts that loop on repeat through your brain, day in and day out, holding you back from moving forward. Being stuck has become pervasive and threatens to overwhelm our work lives. As you talk to colleagues, your team, and others in your network over the coming weeks, notice how often the conversation veers toward topics of being stuck. You'll find that it impacts many people you interact with every day.

A report by tech giant Oracle and Workplace Intelligence titled *State of Work 2022* found that 75 percent of respondents said they feel stuck professionally and 22 percent are too overwhelmed to make any changes. The report also found that feeling stuck at work spills into our personal lives. Seventy percent of people in the study said that feeling stuck at work negatively impacts their personal lives, 40 percent said it also added extra stress and anxiety, and a little more than 25 percent of people said it took focus away from their personal lives.

As you're busy leading your team, building your business, and achieving your goals, you need to stop to recognize how you and your team are succeeding and struggling. There is a strong possibility that many of your team members are feeling stuck. Understanding how to help them, and yourself, get unstuck will provide you with the master leadership tools you can use for the rest of your career. There is much to unpack when we talk about being stuck: many reasons why it happens and many layers to understanding how to keep moving forward.

How Did I Get Here?

You've risen to the position you're in because you can manage yourself and your business. But the aftermath of the pandemic, the impacts of climate change, increased social unrest, and economic instability has only compounded fear, uncertainty, and doubt—or FUD as they call it in the tech industry. Even the most mentally strong leaders can get stuck when they come up against FUD. And seriously, who doesn't come up against one of those feelings at least once per day? Unfortunately, FUD makes many professionals freeze or want to run from problems or experience heightened anxiety. When our thoughts are taken up with so much that is unknown, I see leaders use short-term thinking, scarcity mentality, and protection tactics to make it through each day. I'm here to help make you aware of that thinking. You can't afford to let fear, uncertainty, and doubt stunt your team and your business.

Thanks to advances in neuroscience, we now know exactly how your brain reacts to negative thoughts and overload. Let's look at one emotion, fear, and the impact it has on body and brain. You can recognize fear by the sensations it creates in your body. Your breathing starts getting faster, and then your heart rate follows. Your muscles start to tighten up; many people feel it in their jaw tightening. You may feel hot in your face, palms, or back of your neck. Your mouth might feel dry, and your vision might narrow down. This is a lot of physical reaction for one feeling.

When your brain perceives something that causes fear or stress, it triggers automatic physiological reactions that are known as the fight-or-flight response. This activates your sympathetic nervous system, which Harvard Health describes as functioning like a gas pedal in a car. The sympathetic nervous system triggers the fight-or-flight response, providing your body with a burst of energy so that it can respond to perceived dangers. If stress or fear continues, the burst of energy turns into an always-on engine in your body. Unfortunately, over time this response has the potential to erode health and create problems like high blood pressure, heart issues, a potential for stroke, and more. Brain scientists can help us understand the optimal state for being able to move from fear to safety and put us back in control of our bodies and brains.

An article from Harvard Health outlines three ways to counter stress and fear responses. The first is creating your own relaxation responses: "These include deep abdominal breathing, focus on a soothing word (such as peace or calm), visualization of tranquil scenes, repetitive prayer, yoga, and tai chi." The second is incorporating regular physical activity into your life such as walking, lifting weights, running, or practicing tai chi. The last way is creating systems of social support around yourself so that you can connect with others whom you feel good around and who care for you.

Leaders in the tech industry are just like you. They face seemingly insurmountable challenges, must lead teams when times are uncertain, and they face plenty of fear, uncertainty, and doubt. They have also studied brain science, biohacking social science, and in recent years have started to create an ecosystem that supports wellness as a business advantage.

Recognizing the Signs

Recognizing the early signs of being stuck is an important step toward positive action. The faster you recognize the signs of hesitation, resistance, and distraction, the faster you can pull yourself back to the direction you were traveling or move into a new lane. Here are some classic signs you or someone you work with may be getting stuck:

1 Not meeting goals and no longer caring

2 Becoming distracted by a new idea or many new ideas

3 Digging deep into one area of the business and being unable to pull yourself out to look at the bigger picture

4 Becoming overly negative and/or critical in thinking and thoughts

5 Distracting yourself with anything other than what you should be focused on

6 Starting to add new projects to your list even though important projects aren't finished

7 Not doing the work on your mindset, physical health, or things that once brought you happiness

8 Starting to feel more fear and fear of failing

9 Procrastinating

10 Feeling helpless and unsure of how to move forward

11 Blaming others for lack of progress

12 Feeling jealous often and ruminating on why things are so easy for others and not for you

Maybe you already know the signs that happen before you are fully stuck. Often these are a combination of behaviors, thoughts, and actions (or inaction) that come together to create a slowdown in momentum until you feel that there are too many roadblocks to keep moving forward. Take a few minutes now and note which of the signs of stalling mentioned above reflect your situation. Or grab your tablet or a pen and paper and add to the list so that you have something to refer to in the future. If you're ready to have a conversation with your team about the challenges of being stuck, you can brainstorm a list together. This is a great step to creating understanding and to supporting a culture of helping each other stay unstuck.

Mental Health Check

The tech industry is not historically known for its concern for mental health. Working in tech was mostly about hustle culture, nonstop relentlessness leading to the big payoffs. In some companies, this has led to a culture of misconduct and abuse. And sometimes these cultures are celebrated, idolized, and viewed as the only path to creating a billion-dollar company. But the truth is that for the hard-working individuals who feel chewed up from working in these cultures, the effect on mental health is debilitating.

The Center for Workplace Mental Health, part of the American Psychiatric Association Foundation, studies and publishes data on mental health in American workplaces. The foundation's data from mid-2020 shows that 8 percent of the population experienced anxiety issues in the first half of 2019, and that by mid-2020, 31 percent of the population was experiencing anxiety. The data for depression is equally as concerning. Seven percent of the population experienced depression issues in the first half of 2019, and by mid-2020, it had spiked to 25 percent. Anxiety and depression in Black Americans rose more quickly and at higher rates than any other race in the study.

The effects of depression and anxiety are enormous for our families, communities, and workplaces. The sharp increase in the number of people impacted by depression and anxiety is why I believe that mental wellness will be a key area of business focus for the decades ahead for both the tech industry and the global business community. Ignoring the connection between mental health and work has real business impact with lost productivity and increasing health care costs.

Mental health issues are different from common roadblocks and stalls, and they are even more important to identify as the tools I am offering here might not be enough. If you are unsure if what you're experiencing and feeling is healthy, please seek help from a medical or mental health professional. I've listed some resources in the back of the book.

Where Are You Headed?

When I talk with leaders who are stuck, they often say they feel like something is missing in their lives. They want more but have no idea what. They list around like a ship in a storm, reeling from one idea to another and wondering each time if they've found what they're searching for. That empty feeling or longing sensation is common, even for those who look wildly successful and like they've got it all. Success doesn't prevent you from not knowing what you want in the future, and it doesn't prevent you from getting help in figuring it out.

I always believed that what I wanted was somewhere out in the world, and that if I read enough, searched enough, and talked to enough people, I would find what I was looking for. In some ways, this has been true. Voracious reading has brought me new ideas and techniques and almost always leaves me inspired. People I value have asked me important questions that have prompted realizations that I hadn't thought possible. However, it was my chiropractor who shifted my external quest to an internal one.

My chiropractor is not typical. He knows what is hot in tech. He knows who is funded and by how much. He invests in a venture capital fund or two; he knows who's launching new start-ups, and who is poaching whom from which company. He knows what *Fast Company*'s cover story will be in three months, and he told me that SPACs (special purpose acquisition company) were the next hot stock trend before it was picked up in the media. This guy is all tech all the time because his clients all work in the tech industry and share what they know with him.

He is also deep into mindfulness, spirituality, and Buddhism (as are many in the tech industry; I'll talk more about this in chapter 7). He is also a yogi, and one night I attended his monthly yoga class. The class was light on yoga and heavy on Buddhist concepts, which was fine by me; I was open to learning something new. During the class, he described one concept of completeness. He explained the base concept that we are all Buddha, and since we are all Buddha, we are already complete. We have everything we need in us already.

When he said this, my eyes popped open and I almost screamed, "What!"

I have always searched so hard outside myself to figure out who I should become, what I wanted, and how I could be successful. But here was this person telling me that whatever I was to become was already within me, and my work was to integrate knowledge, experience, understanding, awareness, and healing so that I could bring forward myself. When you consider the idea that everything you will ever be and have and will achieve is already inside you, and that your work is to gently uncover this as you move through your life, what does that change for you?

This idea shifted my life view. I was still reading everything, but not in a desperate attempt to figure out what was for me and how to move forward. I was happy to read and know that I would find ideas that were meant for me. I felt such peace believing that everything I needed would come in time, and along with that peace came a different confidence than I'd had in the past.

Knowing something is missing is a master signal that you're stuck and that you want something different in your life. Simply put, you are totally normal if you feel that you don't know where you're headed, there are obstacles all around, and you're not sure how to move forward.

Think of it this way: you are in exactly the right place right now. Knowing you are stuck is the first step to solving the problem.

Review Your Values

Part of the work to getting and staying unstuck is knowing what's important to you and understanding how your values guide your life. When was the last time you thought about your values? Can you talk about them with others, make decisions based on them, and understand the role they play in moving you forward at work?

I was in my early thirties before I understood that my values had a connection to the work I do every day. At that time, I was working for a global tech company on a competitive team with a cutthroat culture. Someone on that team was always on the outs, and most of my days were spent trying to move my projects ahead while navigating the politics, egos, and back-stabbing. I loved the work, but every night I was drained with a capital *D*. I had a little girl, a great husband, and aspirations to grow my career, but I didn't know if I had the energy. I felt off a lot and wasn't sure what to do about it.

Around this time, I started my MBA. I took a strategic business redesign class, and I was asked to map my values to my work. The look on my face could not have been more confused. First, I hadn't looked at my values on paper, maybe ever. Working through the pages of example values, I felt energy for words like *independence, ambition, learning,* which I quickly circled. When I then lined up my values with my job responsibilities and how I worked, there were gaping holes. When I reviewed what I had found with my professor, she asked how I felt every day, and I had a lightbulb moment. I felt like shit, and I took that shit home with me.

"Your work is not in alignment with your values," she clarified. I could see that.

"Well, what do I do then?" I asked.

"Get them aligned in your current job or move on to something else," she advised.

That clarity put me on the track to being able to choose roles and goals that are authentic to my values. If I ever start to have that off feeling, I can check back in on how my values align with my work each time.

Your Values Selector

To start the work of being unstuck, you need to know who you are, what matters to you, and how you want to live your life. Look at how your values align with your work. How closely are they lined up? If your response to this is "What are values?" that's okay. Here's an exercise that will help you.

Read through this list of values and circle the ones that are most important to you. You may want to circle ones that sound the best, but instead circle ones that are true to how you want to live your life. I recommend you circle three to six values to start. You can always come back to this section and even add values to this list that you think are missing.

- Achievement
- Adventure
- Ambition
- Authenticity
- Authority
- Autonomy
- Balance
- Beauty
- Boldness
- Challenge
- Citizenship
- Community
- Compassion
- Competency
- Contribution
- Creativity
- Curiosity
- Determination
- Fairness
- Faith

- Fame
- Family
- Friendships
- Fun
- Growth
- Happiness
- Honesty
- Humor
- Independence
- Influence
- Inner harmony
- Integrity
- Justice
- Kindness
- Knowledge
- Leadership
- Learning
- Love
- Loyalty
- Meaningful work

- Openness
- Optimism
- Peace
- Pleasure
- Poise
- Popularity
- Recognition
- Religion
- Reputation
- Respect
- Responsibility

- Security
- Self-respect
- Service
- Spirituality
- Stability
- Status
- Success
- Trustworthiness
- Truthfulness
- Wealth
- Wisdom

Once you have updated yourself on your values, you'll be clear on what's important to you. You can bring that understanding to your work on creating your long-term vision for your business and team. You'll start that work in the next chapter.

Successful People Get Stuck, Too

A few years ago, I noticed a trend with tech companies that were going public on the stock market, which is the ultimate success for the tech start-up set. Most of them had been in business a decade or more. Though the media were covering them as overnight success stories, the founders and their leadership teams had been working and slogging and solving for a long time to get to the point they had reached. When I went back and looked through the history of some of those companies and talked in detail with executives who were leading newly public companies or had gone public a few years earlier, they all shared the hard stories of being stuck, almost packing it all in, and having to figure out how to move forward.

I was part of a tech company that navigated the experience of going public on the stock market. When I started interviewing at this clean tech company, they were pre-IPO and rumored to be filing their S-1 form (the registration a company needs to sell shares on the stock exchange) soon. I couldn't believe I was getting a shot to work with this legendary team who had invented a new solar technology that changed an industry. The founders and executives of the company were ambitious, brilliant, and driven. When I interviewed with one of the founders, he took me through a set of questions that Google uses with its candidates. I was more challenged in those thirty minutes than I'd been in a long time. The CEO was intense in our conversations, with questions so direct and sharp that I felt sure I couldn't intellectually keep up with this team.

I got the job, and over the next few years, I learned much more about their path to the success. The CEO told me that he had been hired by the founders to operationalize the business as they worked to get their tech to market. This was a brand-new technology, and it was slow going to get it into use. As they slogged away at early sales, the company was also burning through a lot of cash, which is common in tech start-ups.

The interests of venture capitalists had cooled on clean tech during that time, conversations were harder to have, calls weren't returned, and they couldn't secure the next round of financial funding. They reached a point of being truly stuck, and the CEO's anxiety was building as the bills continued to roll in. Fortunately, a long-time investor agreed to come in with some more funding. Then a distributor, a big one, agreed to stock the product and train his team on the technology, and a journalist for an important tech publication wrote a prominent article about the company. From there, the momentum built and allowed the company to secure the business and move ahead.

What struck me most about this story was that although the business always looked destined to become a public company and achieve huge financial and business success, the reality was that they were almost stuck many times. But they always worked through it, using specific tools, techniques, and ways of thinking to keep them moving forward.

As you look at, and perhaps even compare yourself to, the success of others, know that they have been stuck, too. There is no success without hard times, and no light without the dark. But I'll show you how to know when the dark is coming, give you tools to work through it so you can get back into the light, and then get ready to move through the whole crazy, happy cycle again.

The UNSTUCK Model

Now that you know that feeling stuck is common and that even the most successful people get stuck at some point, it's time to unveil the highlights of the UNSTUCK model that will guide the rest of our time together in this book. This is just the beginning of getting and keeping you moving forward in your fabulous, ambitious, extraordinary career.

U—Understanding Where You Want to Be

Having a vision of where you want to be is the first step in getting you unstuck. It can also be the hardest step. Some people are worried that if they commit to a vision and a set of goals, they are locked into a defined path and will miss other opportunities. They feel that by leaving all possibilities open, they'll capture everything. In this chapter, we'll work through how to develop your vision and identify the benefits for you and your business in having a long-term vision to work from.

N—New Thinking

Tech companies are abundant with new thinking. Tech leaders have developed the ability to see around corners and constantly develop new ideas as they advance toward their vision. We'll explore how to do new thinking on purpose and use proven methods to develop new ideas that can lead to breakthroughs.

S—Short-Term Tentative Goals

Can you think of at least three books that you own that are all about goal setting? It is a big topic, and I can tell you that we've all been doing it wrong. Did you know that only 9 percent of people who set New Year's resolutions achieve them? That is a terrible result for the biggest goal-setting moment of the year. Setting short-term tentative goals may be a new idea for you, and in this chapter, we'll cover the fundamentals of tentative goal setting, methods to communicating those tentative goals to activate your business, and why it can help you achieve more in the long run.

T—Think and Act Big

I speak with hundreds of start-ups, scale-ups, and successful leaders each year who know this tech secret. You need to be in the world acting as a big brand and company long before you've reached traditional milestones of success. Building a perception and buzz about your company supports meeting important growth goals, attracts the right talent, and helps you break through when you're unknown. In this chapter, we'll look at the ways you can confidently think and act big, with lessons from tech's challenger brands.

U—Unusual Moves

Most of us have been following established business play-books, and it's time to make some unusual moves. Tech leaders experiment and try new ideas. They create unexpected partnerships, sometimes with their competitors! And I've seen them rip up entire business lines to invest in new products, all based on client feedback. In this chapter, I'll share some of the most unusual moves to inspire you to find new ideas in your industry and business.

C—Creating New

Creating new is what the tech industry does best. Companies create new categories, companies, products, and services by coupling big visions with action, always with the goal of moving forward. This doesn't mean creating something new is a straight path. In the tech industry, failures are seen as part of the journey to success. Sometimes when an idea isn't quite the right one for the business, pivoting becomes the roadmap to help you keep going. Tech leaders are also at the forefront of using tools like meditation and biohacking so that they can continue creating new.

K—Keep Going

No matter what comes your way, when you are unstuck, you can always keep going forward. To keep going, you will need to know when you might be sabotaging your progress and how to find the wins in the process of staying unstuck. I want you to know how to celebrate all the small and big wins along the way. Most high performers wait until the final success to celebrate, but we're going to look at why and how you should celebrate throughout the journey and share what you're building and learning with others along the way.

I HOPE YOU ARE FEELING EXCITED, ready, and supported knowing that almost all high performers have been stuck but that there is a tested and proven model you can use to start moving yourself and your business forward. Today is the day you start to become unstuckable by taking the insights from thousands of successful tech companies and applying it to your business. Let's go!

2

UNDER STANDING

WHERE YOU WANT TO BE

"I want to put a ding in the universe."
STEVE JOBS, co-founder of Apple

TECH LEGEND Ben Horowitz is co-founder and general partner at venture capital firm Andreessen Horowitz, and he is also the author of *The Hard Things About Hard Things*, a handbook for tech founders, leaders, and CEOs. Prior to becoming an author and venture capitalist, Horowitz was co-founder and CEO of tech company Opsware (formerly LoudCloud). In his book, Horowitz details the hard work of creating, building, saving, and selling his company to Hewlett-Packard for $1.6 billion. The power of his vision has carried him through all stages of his leadership, and he believes it's even more important when times are hard.

"Can the leader articulate a vision that's interesting, dynamic, and compelling?" said Horowitz. "More important, can the leader do this when things fall apart? More specifically, when the company gets to a point when it does not make financial sense for any employee to continue working there, will the leader be able to articulate a vision that's compelling enough to make people stay?"

In my polls of business leaders, only about a quarter of them have a long-term vision. When I ask how well their teams understand the company's vision and can also talk about it, the percentage drops to about 10 percent. Although those leaders might have goals for the year that are for revenue or profit, they don't really know where they want to be. They have no vision that extends over a three-year period or longer. And they couldn't tell you why what they are working on matters to them, why it should matter to their team, and how it adds to the good of the world.

A decade ago, none of that was important. The pursuit of growth and profit was reason enough for a company to exist. But this is no longer a sustainable business perspective. The rise of the purpose-driven consumer, and their expectations of the businesses they buy from and work for, has changed how business leaders approach the values, purpose, and vision of their organizations.

Taking insight from hundreds of tech leaders, we know that those who are successful have a clear, compelling vision of where they want to be. They may have an epiphany about a hole in the market, the imagination to create an entirely new product or service, or they decide to join an emerging industry to make their mark. No matter what business they imagine, create, or build, they start with the vision, which articulates where they want to be.

In this chapter, you will work on discovering where you want to be and learn about the steps to building that vision. You may be tempted to skip over this work and get right to the ideas for implementing and executing your vision, but if do, you'll miss this powerful and foundational step of the UNSTUCK model.

Start with the End

Setting a vision for the long term is key to making the impact in the world that you want to make. It gives you a direction to aim for and can be a powerful motivator to keep you unstuck as the natural challenges of business come up. A vision also captures the attention and imagination of your team, your customers, partners, and prospects. It creates a magnetic force: others want to know more about your business and what you're trying to achieve.

Marc Benioff, founder of Salesforce, saw all these benefits to creating a vision when he started his company. In his book *Behind the Cloud*, he writes about having a big dream. "I believed that all software would eventually be delivered in the cloud. I would soon find that to pursue my dream, I had to believe in it passionately and be ready to constantly defend it. This lesson learned during our earliest days still guides us today."

The vision that you create or refine or redefine should be one that will take you years to achieve. It should be aspirational and a summary of what you want your business or team to be, achieve, or create. It describes what you are working toward in the future, together, and the positive impact you'll have in the world.

It may take you a few weeks or a few months to create your vision. You may refine your vision over time as you get input from important people in and around your business.

There are a few activities you can do that will give you inspiration, ideas, and motivation on the journey to create the vision of where you want to be.

Get Curious

One of the most frequent questions I get is "How do I figure out where I want to be?" This is usually asked with exasperation or sadness, and often by leaders who run very successful businesses but are feeling stuck. Getting started can be overwhelming, and there are many more pressing issues facing you every day. You can begin with small steps, with small actions like noticing what excites you.

When you are charting your vision, start by getting deeply curious about what's happening in your business and life. Start looking for trends, themes, and insights by noticing what is already around you. Which companies do you admire most, and more importantly, why do admire them? Look at competitors, adjacent businesses in your industry, and trend forecasts from analysts covering your space and media headlines. Review your customer lists, upcoming initiatives, projects you're going ahead with, and those you aren't. All of this can give you inspiration for writing a long-term vision statement for your business.

Move on to social media and look at all your channels, not only work ones like LinkedIn. If you're on TikTok, Discord, Snapchat, look at those as well. Inspiration comes from all areas of your life. Review who you're following. Why are you following them? This exercise could lead to you cleaning up your social media channels, which isn't a bad outcome either. Ask yourself who you are inspired by and why you are inspired by them. Write their names down with your observations.

Which events will you go to over the next year? Or which events are dream events that you think are out of your reach but you'd love to be part of? I know this line of questioning is repetitive, but investigating why you are attracted to people, ideas, companies, concepts, and patterns can provide insight into the direction you want to take your business.

In this work, you are looking for information that creates an emotion in you that feels exciting and is a long-term challenge. I know you already put together strategy for your business and know how to use data and tools like SWOT analyses. Tech leaders do business planning, too, and those who are incredibly successful first have a compelling vision to make sure they remain unstuck.

I recommend you make these observations over a two- to three-week period, making notes each day on what you notice.

If you are working on this with your team, ask them to do the same so that you all come together with observations that can be shared. This is all input you can use to create your long-term vision.

Constructive Envy

Envy often comes from a negative place. But envy can be a positive if you turn it upside down and transform it into inspiration. You can use it to find direction and push yourself into action.

The first time I remember being deeply envious was when I was a few years into the workforce and my boss invited me to dinner at her place. She had a great condo in the middle of the city, and I thought about how much I also wanted to have a home like that someday instead of the tiny basement apartment I was sharing with my then boyfriend.

That envy sat with me for weeks. Finally, I thought I should look up how much a home like that would cost so I would know for the future. It turned out that it wasn't as expensive as I thought, and that it was, in fact, within reach. I was shocked and started going to open houses, talking to realtors, and researching how to get a mortgage. It wasn't until a few years later that I realized that all that envy had moved me into action, and being moved into action was a magical thing.

When I feel envious of someone, I step back and look at what that envy is telling me about what I want and the direction I should be headed in. Examining my envy has led me to some major direction setting and goals through my career.

Another time the green-eyed monster struck was when I was at Web Summit, a big tech event held in Europe annually. At that time, it was a new, very hot event with hundreds of speakers. I watched the stage fill and refill with keynotes and panels and fireside chat conversations. I felt envious of those on stage in front of hundreds of their tech peers and the most important media in the industry. They were in positions of influence and building brands for themselves and their companies. That envy burned hot through the rest of the conference and on the eleven-hour plane ride home. Because I can't sleep on a plane, I spent that time looking at the envy and seeing that the gap for me was confidence and thinking big. I hadn't been thinking big enough for my business or career, and I certainly didn't have the confidence to be on stage at an event like Web Summit.

A professor at INSEAD, one of the top global graduate business schools, calls this constructive envy. He defines constructive envy as "... situations whereby people admire the person envied which includes the wish to become like them. In this form, envy signals an unfilled need and can turn into a great motivating force." He notes that under certain circumstances, envy can be a good thing.

Once I saw the gap, I knew what I wanted and how it fit in with the vision I had for my work and team, and it helped me set a new direction of where I want to go. Having the confidence to put myself forward on big stages and increase my influence in the industry was now part of the vision. That feeling of envy pushed me to get clear on what I wanted and then move forward to seeing it through.

Let's dig deeper. Think back to the last time you envied someone. Answer these questions:

- When does the feeling of envy come up for you?
- When you sit back and think about someone else whose life you admire, who comes to mind?
- What is it about their life that you envy and inspires you?
- What insights about yourself can you develop based on what you're noticing?

Once you've spent some time on the questions, consider one thing you can do to move your envy into healthy action so that you can get where you want to be.

Crossover Inspiration

Though I've worked in the tech industry my entire career, I have always sought out sources of inspiration from other industries and disciplines that have put me in front of new thinking and ideas. Whatever it is that interests you personally is a great place to start.

Far Analogies

Famed Silicon Valley venture capitalist Bill Gurley has funded and worked with some of the most successful tech companies in the world, such as OpenTable, Uber, Stitch Fix, and Zillow. Gurley cites the work of Dr. Keith Holyoak, a cognitive psychologist and professor at UCLA, who studies far analogies, which is the idea of smart people borrowing ideas from other disciplines far away from and outside of their own area of expertise: "a lot of the breakthroughs in science have come from people that have changed disciplines or changed genres. If you study science and history, the biggest breakthroughs come from those people that have a different mental framework and move over and then see things differently."

If you apply the concept of far analogies to your own life, you may also find crossover ideas that inspire your vision. For example, I love to travel and subscribe to all the travel magazines and newsletters. I often get ideas for my business by reading what's new and happening in these resources.

One idea that inspired me years ago was a feature story on designers in residence who worked with an upscale hotel each quarter to bring a new design style to life in the hotel's rooms. Looking around the tech industry to see if there was something similar, I saw that venture capital firms were launching entrepreneurs in residence programs to bring new people and ideas to their organizations. I could see that by partnering with leaders in their industries, companies could improve their brands and inspire their team and customers. This idea made its way into my thinking about the company vision my team was working on at that time.

Let's dig deeper:

- What interests do you have outside your work life?
- Have you seen ideas from other industries used by people in your network?
- Are there one or two topics or ideas you've seen from your outside work interests that could be adapted to your business?
- If there is one idea that is interesting but you're not sure it could work in your business, explore how it could be used by journaling or sketching out the idea.
- What are some of the benefits that can be gained from using ideas from other sectors and industries?

The Audio Explosion

It is safe to say that if you're constantly consuming the same content, you're eventually going to hit an inspiration plateau. But the explosion in audio platforms has created easy ways to search out what's happening in other industries and be inspired with new ideas. Podcast Index reports more than 4 million podcasts in its index with content from every industry and topic under the sun. You don't need to watch another webinar, but you can listen to a podcast at your leisure.

Twitter Spaces, Clubhouse, and Stereo are social audio apps that take advantage of the demand for new content. These audio platforms also allow anyone to sign up and host an event where they talk about a topic and take questions from the audience.

Take some time to explore and listen to content and speakers you don't usually hear from, and note any insights they share that you'll add to the vision input list.

Let's dig deeper:

- What new sources of audio content could you listen to?
- Once you've explored some new sources, what are one to three surprising new ideas or insights you heard?
- Is there a way to infuse the trend of audio into your long-term vision?

Visualizing Future You

The next step in understanding where you want to be is creating a clear picture of a future version of yourself. Though your vision work is for the company or team, this exercise is personal. Finding your place in the future with a version of yourself that is beyond who you are today will bring you clarity while creating the vision for your company or team.

The first time I heard of a similar technique was in Jack Canfield's book *The Success Principles*. Although I can't remember how exactly this book arrived in my life, it was transformational, and it's the book I have gifted the most. At the time that I read *The Success Principles*, I had college debt equivalent to two years' salary, and I was so behind on my payments that a debt collector tracked me down, threatened to call my company's CEO, and garnish my wages. It scared me enough to get my act together and start figuring out how to be a responsible adult.

As I read Canfield's book, I stopped for a long time on a chapter called "Act As If." The concept he introduced was that I should act as if I was already my future self and create space to play out that future. One of the examples he gives is about meeting a seminar leader who had just returned from working in Australia. Canfield was so inspired from the meeting that he decided he wanted to be an international consultant and added this to his vision of himself. In his vision, he decided that working in Australia would be his first target. He got posters showing Australia's popular destinations, ordered business cards with the title "international consultant" on them, and every day imagined being in Australia. Within a year, he was invited to work in multiple cities in Australia. He describes it as the Law of Attraction at work. "The Law of Attraction simply states that like attracts like. The more you create the vibration—the mental and emotional states—of already having something, the faster you attract it to you. This is an immutable law of the universe and critical to accelerating your rate of success."

I know that sometimes this "future you" exercise can cause people to hesitate or freeze up. You might be concerned that by committing yourself to a vision a few years out, you'll miss another opportunity in the process. Creating a vision of yourself in the future isn't a static exercise. You can adjust the vision over time and use it as a tool to bring to life the vision you're setting for your business and life. I promise that no one is going to hold you to every idea you put down about future you!

There are many ways to develop the future you picture. Here are specific ideas I've seen work well for leaders.

Think Ahead

First, I am a big fan of developing a three-year outlook and encourage you to use that timeframe as you create future you. Three years is the preferred timeframe because it's far enough out that you can create a very ambitious vision of yourself, but it's also not too far in the future that you can't imagine it in full. I've included an exercise in this chapter to help you do that.

Draw It Out

Some people want to get out a vision board and use images from magazines to create a visual representation of their future. If that is a fun way for you to do this, then go for it. Others may want to use a big sketch pad and draw and write to express themselves. A private Pinterest board is another tool you can use, or many leaders journal their vision and come back to their writing again and again.

Acknowledge Your Ambition

I've also worked with people who feel scared to admit to themselves how ambitious they are by writing down something that they see as out of reach right now.

One tech executive I know had a hard time getting specific about the kind of accomplishments he could imagine achieving three years from now. After a lot of questions and cajoling, he finally blurted out that he aspired to be on *Fast Company*'s 100 Most Creative People list. He looked embarrassed and started making statements about how he knew it was a crazy ambition and not possible. We dug into why including this goal as part of his future vision made him feel so terrible. He finally admitted that he was scared about what his parents would think.

It turns out that he immigrated to the US with his parents when he was one year old. Their philosophy was put your head down, work hard, don't wish for too much, and make your family proud by having a steady job and a good life. In the past, when he voiced big dreams, one of his parents would say, "Don't you have enough? Just be happy that you have a good job with good pay." Their worldview shaped how he thought about himself, and as a result, he had gotten good and stuck in the current stage of his career. Together, we discovered that to become unstuck, he would need to create a new future version of himself, which was uncomfortable to articulate but would serve his vision, values, and ambition. His story may sound familiar to you, or you may have your own story about what is holding you back from starting to create a future you. I want you to acknowledge how uncomfortable it feels and then get busy doing it anyway.

Get Comfortable with Being Uncomfortable

Speaking of being uncomfortable, to get unstuck, you must get used to feeling uncomfortable and then taking the next step anyway. This is a mantra I use often, sometimes every day! I'll repeat to myself, "I'm scared and I'm doing it anyway." By saying this, it doesn't take away the feeling of being scared, but naming what I feel and saying I'm doing it anyway helps me build confidence.

For most her career, Ginni Rometty worked at IBM, with her last eight years spent as president, CEO, and chair. She recently added author to her resume with her book, *Good Power: Leading Positive Change in Our Lives, Work, and World.* At a Fortune Most Powerful Women event, she was asked to talk about how she continues to reinvent herself and her business. She talked about taking on assignments before she thought she was ready and the hard moments in business that helped her grow. Then she summarized her point in this statement: "Growth and comfort do not coexist. They cannot exist together." Hearing her clearly state that you can't grow in times of comfort may help you normalize any uneasy feelings you might have about creating your future.

Years ago, I was working on my own future self, and that vision included a CEO title. I had a great supporter in my boss, who was the global CEO of the business I was with, but I hadn't told her about my future me vision. Through building the profile of the business, I was doing a lot of press, mostly feature stories on leadership in tech, and a reporter asked me where I saw my career in a few years. I blurted out, "I want to be CEO." My next thought was *Oh shit, I said it out loud.* I hadn't gone into that conversation planning to talk about future me, but I ended up doing that anyway. The article headline ended up being that quote, which made me very uncomfortable because now everyone who read it could see I was ambitious. Then I thought, *Fuck it. This is what I want and now it's in the universe.* Eighteen months later, I was promoted and given the CEO title.

Keep Track

Some tech leaders like to get specific right away about what they need to do to achieve the future version of themselves and start mapping out the goals in spreadsheets. Each month they check in on their progress, sometimes giving themselves scores out of one hundred or using a system of red, yellow, green. If mapping out goals at the beginning of this process motivates you, go ahead and do this, though it's certainly not a requirement at this stage. Assessing how you're doing will keep you honest about the progress you're making, so use a system that works for you.

Your Three-Year Outlook

Now it's time for you to create a vision statement for your business or team and future you with a three-year outlook. If you have trouble with this at first, remember that there are no wrong answers here; everything can be crossed out or deleted. You need to start putting something down to get going! So, stop stressing, take a deep breath, lower your shoulders down from your ears, and start to dream.

Using the three-year outlook above, let's start with the basics of future you:

1 Who are you personally:
   - What age are you?
   - How does that make you feel?
   - Where do you live?
   - Do you have a partner?
   - Do you have children? If so, what ages are they?
   - Where do your siblings and/or parents live?
   - What kind of home do you live in?
   - What routine do you have each day?
   - What do you do for fun?
   - What is the state of your physical and mental health?
   - Who are the most important people in your life?
   - What experiences are you having or creating in your life?
   - What have you achieved that makes you proud?
   - How are you sharing what you know with others?
   - What are you looking forward to in the next stage of growth?
   - How much time do you spend with family, friends, community, and work?
   - What has brought you the most satisfaction and peace in your life?

2 Now let's move into vision creation that you'll use for your business or team:
- What business(es) are you in?
- What clients or customers do you have?
- What products or services do you offer?
- What problems do you solve for your industry?
- How much revenue are you making?
- What is your profit margin?
- What skills do your employees have?
- Why do prospective employees want to work with you?
- What does it feel like to start work every day?
- Who do you partner with and why?
- How do you spend each day?
- What is your team accomplishing?
- Where are you positioned in the market?
- What do your clients/customers say about you?
- How do others in your industry (competitors, analysts, prospects, industry leaders) think of you?
- Where are you speaking?
- What industry associations are you part of, and how do you participate with them?
- Why do people seek out your team?
- What is the long-term positive impact you're making on your industry or the wider business world?
- What have you created that has changed your industry?

With your answers to these questions, you can shape a vision that's inspiring and aspirational. For future you, summarize in a few sentences who you want to be, how you want to live, and why it's important. For your business vision, summarize what you want your business to do, how you will do it, and why it's important.

IN TRUTH, UNDERSTANDING where you want to be and creating a compelling vision for your business is a complex, emotional journey that has no right answer. If you're at this point, I hope you take comfort in knowing that most people are at this stage. The great news is that you're now well equipped with the tools you need to work yourself through this first part of the journey to being unstuck.

When you start by being curious, you open up your thinking to what you are already interested in and what naturally captures your energy and time. By using the feeling of envy, you can identify what you would like to incorporate into your business and personal life. Using far analogies and inspiration from everywhere can help you find insights and ideas that push you into bigger visions and breakthrough ideas. Lastly, working on a version of future you can help you place yourself in the creation of a long-term vision for your business.

Creating your vision and understanding where you want to be are critical steps in becoming unstuck, and we will be using it as a reference point throughout the rest of the book. If you have work to do in creating your vision, get that started this week.

Are you ready to move on? If not, stay with this chapter a little longer, and once you have a draft version of your vision, you are ready take the next step and explore how the tech industry uses new thinking.

TL;DR

At the end of the UNSTUCK chapters, I have summarized key points into TL;DR summaries. TL;DR is an acronym that stands for "too long; didn't read" and is used widely in the tech industry to summarize longer communications. The inclusion of these summaries doesn't mean you should skip the chapter and read only this, but you can use this section to refer back to content as you work on keeping unstuck.

- Start with the end in mind. A critical first step in getting unstuck is to sketch out your long-term vision for where you want to be.

- Curiosity and watching when envy comes up are two powerful observation tools that will point you in the right direction.

- Seek inspiration from all parts of your life and bring in insights and ideas from unusual places as you create your long-term vision.

- Developing a clear picture of your future you will anchor you for long-term success.

3

NEW
THINKING

"In limits there is freedom. Creativity thrives within structure."
JULIA CAMERON, author, teacher, and artist

I F THERE IS ONE SKILL that I wish would be added to school curriculum, it is the skill of new thinking. Of course, there are all kinds of important thinking—strategic thinking, critical thinking, conceptual thinking—but new thinking is a special one that's required as the business world continues to shift with the effects of pandemic recovery, impact of recession, demands of digital transformation, societal shifts, consumer expectations, and new ways to work.

In past decades of business, command and control operations was common, and hierarchy ruled. Some industries are still shackled to this model but are now cracking under the pressure of new expectations and requirements. The new model of leadership is about decentralization and empowerment, with every person being a leader of themselves and in service of organizations that align with their values. We're in the early stages of this transformation, and tech leaders have been pressured to adjust their thinking quickly. They are using new thinking to stay ahead.

Many people operate under the assumption that they'll come up with an innovative idea while on a run, in the shower, or doing something totally different from work. And that can absolutely be true. However, it doesn't provide a good framework for you and your team to access innovative thinking regularly. This needs practice, just like any other practice you do to build a skill. New thinking is about being deliberate and structured, which will lead to all kinds of unexpected and inspired ideas.

I love the quotation from author Julia Cameron that opens this chapter because it's counterintuitive. How can structure allow for creativity? Because it focuses the mind on the wonderful creative work and not on the messy process or routine parts. When you know what you're operating within, you can get to the fun faster.

As you work on becoming unstuck, you will become more purposeful with your thoughts. Maybe more purposeful than you've ever been, even though I already know that you're a high achiever and have an expert level of knowledge about your mindset. There is a next click up, though, and I'm going to take you there. You are going to be able to choose and explore different thinking concepts and use them to your advantage.

The tech industry uses many more types of thinking than I cover here, with new models and systems being created and shared continuously. Beyond what's in this chapter, two models you may want to explore further are design thinking and systemic inventive thinking, and I've included information on resources for them in the back of the book.

You can mix and match the new thinking tools explored next, depending on the challenge you need to work through. We're going to cover associational thinking, concrete thinking, critical thinking, and fantasy thinking. All offer a path to new and different ideas. Then I'll take you through the horizons framework to explore how adding time span and innovation planning to how you think can give you a trajectory to reach your long-term vision.

Associational Thinking

This is one of my absolute favorite ways of thinking (although I hope that confession will not bias you against the others in this chapter). The American Psychological Association defines associative thinking as "a relatively uncontrolled cognitive activity in which the mind wanders without specific direction among elements, based on their connections (associations) with one another, as occurs during reverie, daydreaming, and free association." Using this definition as a starting point, you can think of associational thinking as drawing connections between questions, problems, or ideas from unrelated areas. I find associational thinking is best done with a pen and paper or on a tablet that allows you to sketch out words and shapes and draw connections between them.

To do this thinking, you'll need to let your mind wander and pull in thoughts from everywhere, for example, what you've read, watched, talked to people about, listened to, past and current experiences, and people you admire. There is no space off limits for your brain to wander through when you do this work. It's the very opposite of meditating, when you're clearing the mind to focus on here and now. This is about letting your brain gallop around with lots of information.

How to Use Associational Thinking

To illustrate how to use these new ways of thinking, I'll use the example of a marketing leader who is responsible for developing, launching, and marketing a new online class for IT leaders across industries.

Our marketing leader, in this example, takes out a blank sheet of paper and decides to use associational thinking to come up with some ideas. They start writing words that they like. *Music. Magazines. Drums. Beats. Teachers.* They start to remember their favorite teacher from middle school who encouraged them to try new things. Their mind wanders to the online cooking class they took a few weeks ago where they learned how to make truffle mac and cheese, and Snoop Dog showed up for ten minutes as a surprise guest. Then holy shit, their brain pops because they can see the connections between these ideas and how they can market the new class. They know that the target audience is also into music, especially drums, because they had some market research already done on IT managers. They're going to incorporate drumming into the classes and use that as part of the marketing, but also investigate if they can hire a notable industry drummer to do a cameo appearance. They've just used associational thinking to work through a challenge and come up with a tentative plan.

This is thinking you can do alone or with your team. Sometimes you create new ideas in a first session, and sometimes you need to come back to the work a few times to continue adding in thoughts and inspiration. Because it's broad thinking, you will end up with some ideas that seem impossible. Don't discount any of the ideas too quickly. Leaders in tech keep moving forward by coming up with impossible ideas and working on them to see what's possible.

Concrete Thinking

If you are tempted to skip this section because you're not a numbers person, resist the urge and stick with me. I was a classic hates-numbers person and barely passed grade ten math. I did an arts undergrad degree because I didn't want to go near any class that had an equation in it. When I started my MBA and I had no choice but to learn how to source and analyze data, my business world opened up. You can learn how to do concrete thinking and use it to advance your UNSTUCK mindset. Like anything else, it takes practice, and I'd argue that it's a core skill for leadership to have and to be able to hire for.

With concrete thinking, you're going to gather information from different sources and then review it all to develop insights. The information can be any of these plus hundreds more ideas, depending on what challenge in your business you're working on: analyst reports, public company annual reports, trade association trend reports, government reports, national job numbers, rankings, data from your industry that shows sizes of various companies, competitors' websites, your own customer satisfaction and/or employee satisfaction surveys, marketplace analysis, media reports, etc.

How to Use Concrete Thinking

Keeping with the same example I talked about in associational thinking, the marketing leader is now going to tackle the same problem but this time using concrete thinking. What would that look like?

First, they find data on the IT manager. They look at LinkedIn and search for people with the title of IT manager and find there are about 4.5 million people with this title. Then they pull a study from a marketing agency that reports in detail how IT managers get their information and what news media and social outlets they use. This detailed information is all based on a survey that agency did.

The marketing leader reads in that study that Reddit and YouTube are the most popular social channels for the target audience. The study also says that when IT managers are outside of work, music, in particular drumming, is where they spend their time. But they also like fixing up their cars and hanging with their kids. Lastly, when the marketing leader looks at analyst reports from Gartner and Forrester, there is a data point that says about 75 percent of IT managers can authorize a purchase under $500 without senior manager approval. This is all fact-based information that leads the marketing leader to some initial conclusions. So, they set a goal of acquiring 5 percent of the market of 4.5 million people over three years. They select their launch marketing channels as Reddit and YouTube and set the price of the class under $500 so that the prospects don't need to get approval. Now, granted this isn't an entire business or marketing plan, but this concrete information is part of the equation. The process of reading, gathering, and analyzing information allows them to stay unstuck.

In the tech industry, start-ups operate a lot on vision and instinct. As they mature, their leaders move to incorporate more concrete understanding of their markets and audiences so that they can scale their business. Just like tech leaders who use this tool, you can use it to keep moving forward.

Critical Thinking

If you've taken strategy or analysis classes, you've probably developed skills in this area already. But give this critical thinking a chance, as I've adapted this model to today's work pressures and evolved leadership models.

There is a specific path to follow when using critical thinking, which I've outlined here. I'll return to the example of our marketing manager to show you critical thinking in action. This structure was first introduced to me by Jane Lorand, CEO and founder of Catalytic Thinking Labs who I learned business redesign from at Dominican University. She inspired me to integrate it into my work in tech and to share it with others who need tools for meeting complex challenges that need new thinking.

1. Create opportunity and/or problem statements

You want to get clear on the opportunity that's ahead of you and/or the problem you're trying to solve. This seemingly easy step can get very complicated when you work in groups like your leadership team. Frequently, everyone's interpretation of the opportunity or problem is different, which can be surprising, frustrating, and sometimes hurtful. For example, you think your team is on the same page about what you're working to solve, but everyone disagrees once it's written down, and now you might want to say fuck it to the whole process. Don't.

Trust me, this is a gift in the process of keeping your team unstuck. Do you want your team running around for the next two years trying to solve slightly different problems and then you are wondering why the hell you're not getting traction? No. So write down your most important opportunity or problem statement somewhere—on paper, in a shared document, or in a presentation—so that you can all discuss, debate, and get to agreement.

2. Gather all points of view, assumptions, inferences

For this step, list out the points of view you should take into consideration. (Hint: it will be more than one and could be many.) What assumptions does each of your team members have about what you're working on? Get them to write out their assumptions and share them with each other. Then work with those inferences, which are conclusions drawn from observation or information (but be careful here, because inferences can be the cause of bias, discrimination, and snap judgments). We are in a time when we need to change many systems and patterns, so understanding your inferences and your organization's inferences can help with that.

3. Collect essential information

Your essential information can be drawn from the data you sourced in the critical thinking exercise, but it also can be qualitative. Put together all the information you feel is absolutely critical and ask your team to also gather a similar list of information and then share it with each other.

4. Make tentative conclusions

Using the information from the steps above, you can now put together your tentative conclusions. I use the word *tentative* often (one of the chapters in this book is called "Short-Term Tentative Goals"), but not because I'm afraid of commitment or want you to have excuses for not meeting business goals. I use it because of the scientific understanding that has developed about the brain over the past few decades and the impact of pressure and stress on great performance. We also know that new information can come at any time, and market conditions can change quickly. Or the entire world can shut down in a global pandemic, with a storyline straight out of a horror movie.

I want you to consider a line in the sand. On one side, there are goals and plans that are immovable. On the other side, there are tentative conclusions, with goals and plans that are open to evolve and change and where multiple things can be true. If you operate mostly on the immovable side of the line, imagine yourself stepping over into the other side and into a new way of working.

In the UNSTUCK leadership model, the word *and* becomes important and is used to convey ideas that may seem at odds but aren't. An example of this is an organization that says, "We are an ambitious organization who will beat all the competition, and we use new information to regularly update our strategy."

5. Anticipate the consequences

No matter what action you take, there are consequences. They can be positive, negative, or somewhere in between. If you spend a short time detailing these as a team, you'll be able to head off potentially negative outcomes and create responses in advance to those that might emerge. If you do this work, you and your team will be weighing the consequences of decisions together and deciding how to proceed with common understanding. Do not skip this part, no matter how uncomfortable it feels.

6. Take your initial steps

It's time to take your first steps in laying out what you've detailed into a map the team can follow. This is not a business plan but a new thinking map that can help you work through any challenge or problem that is keeping you stuck.

How to Use Critical Thinking

For this section, I'm going to explore critical thinking using the same business example mentioned previously: to develop, launch, and market a new online class targeted at IT managers across industries.

Business vision	Teach the most critical skills to the next generation of technology leaders.
Opportunity and/or problem statement	Provide leadership training to IT managers to help them progress their career. The problems they face are time restraints and low budget authority.
Points of view, assumptions, inferences	• There are enough IT managers to have a healthy and profitable business. • They want leadership skills that we are teaching. • They will spend the time and have the motivation to take an online course. • They can expense learning to their company for anything under $500. • We assume that we can reach them.
Indispensable information	• Personal information on what they like, who influences them. • Purchase authority limits. • Information on their career aspirations and key skills needed for progression. • CEO sign-off.
Tentative conclusions	• There is a market opportunity to pursue. • There is a need for these skills to progress from manager to the next level. • If we can reach .05 percent of the audience with a price point under $500, we will have a viable, profitable, and exciting business.

Consequences	• If we invest $25,000 into creating and marketing the online course but aren't successful in signing up at least 100 IT managers, we'll lose our investment.
	• If we lose our investment, it will be hard, but it won't have a long-term impact on the company.
	• The implication will be we'll need to hold on new training development until next year and sell our current training. We can live with that.
Initial steps	• Finalize the business plan, bringing together all the information and move ahead with hiring a contract course designer to start course creation.
	• Get first party research from one-on-one interviews with the target audience; ten interviews should be enough.

Fantasy Thinking

In the past, there was little room in business for anything other than hard strategy, hard plans, and hard rules. Well, fuck that. We're throwing a little fantasy thinking into our UNSTUCK toolbox, because we get to make the new rules as unstuck leaders.

Thinking based on fantasy relies on emotion, intuition, imagery, sound, and other sensory notions without applied logic or reasoning. In this work, you allow yourself to imagine anything to unlock structures that keep you constrained. Using the words *what if* can help with this form of thinking.

But before you begin, consider your team. This way of thinking is often foreign to business leaders, so they may object to spending any time on it and consider it a waste of time or unprofessional. For a group who will likely have strong resistance to fantasy thinking, I find it helpful to use associational thinking first. Once you use associational thinking to provide unstructured space for idea creation, you may find the team is more open to fantasy thinking.

How to Use Fantasy Thinking

Set a timer for ten to fifteen minutes. Then pose this question to your team: What if anything was possible?

Going back to our example above—to develop, launch, and market a new online class targeted toward IT managers across industries—explore some fantasy thoughts with the team. Here are some "What if" thoughts that might emerge:

- What if the course caught the attention of the most well-known IT people in the industry and they started to talk about it?
- What if we were approached to do a reality TV show about building our company?
- What if we turned the course into a book and it became an international bestseller?
- What if we created a new way of learning that became the standard around the world?
- What if Microsoft made an offer to buy our company because so many of their team were taking our courses?

This thinking is meant to unstick your brain and come up with wild ideas that may never happen but give you energy and some confidence that helps you stay unstuck.

Horizon Thinking

This model was introduced to me by my friend Steven Hoffman, founder of Human Synergy. It's a McKinsey model that's been adapted frequently. Steven introduced it to me because I was frustrated with short-term thinking in my business and hated the Groundhog Day feeling of repeatedly dealing with the same issues while struggling to move quickly on more innovative opportunities.

To get started, find a piece of paper or grab a tablet and draw a table like the one below.

VISION:

Horizon 1	Horizon 2	Horizon 3

When McKinsey rolled out the three-horizon model, each horizon covered a timeframe. Horizon 1 was the closest to the present, covering anywhere from six to twelve months, and horizon 3 was the furthest into the future, potentially years.

However, in this adaptation you can also look at each horizon as a step in innovation thinking, from incremental innovations in horizon 1 to industry disruptive innovations in horizon 3. Then you can also add in timeframes in each horizon. Depending on the speed at which you need to deliver as a business, the ideas in horizon 3 may get delivered in a short window, while incremental innovations documented in horizon 1 may not need to be delivered for a longer period.

Whether you want to use the tool as a timeframe or a scale of innovation, the three-horizon model will break you out of day-to-day thinking and keep you working forward. Let me show you how to use this thinking in both ways.

How to Use Horizon Thinking for Timeframe Planning

Horizon 1: Your short-term plan

Here is where you are going to figure out what needs to happen in the next twelve months to reach your three-year vision located in the horizon 3 box.

Focus on big initiatives that may take a quarter or two to complete and drop them in here. In your first cut of this, the list may be long and consist of a combination of some daily tactics and true initiatives. Don't judge yourself. The main goal of this exercise is to get the ideas down. If you're leading a team or an entire business, bring your leadership team together to work on this so that you're helping them stay unstuck as well.

Horizon 2: Your mid-term plan

In year two of fulfilling your vision, you may struggle to fill in the most important initiatives right away, and that's okay. Allow your mind to wander and use other sections of this book to generate ideas. The ideas that you do fill in here will need more investigation, but this doesn't need to be done now, so don't worry about getting too detailed. You are likely going to change these initiatives as you work throughout year one anyway. Remember, you're not setting these plans in stone. The structure of this model allows you to be creative and in charge of what you will take on.

Horizon 3: The home stretch

Again, this will be a smaller list, as it's hard to know exactly what you'll need to work on in that horizon. But you should still have two or three ideas about what you'll do in that final year to complete your vision.

When working with leadership teams, I find it very effective to sketch out the first version of the horizon template on a big sticky note or giant pieces of paper and then to pull it out quarterly in leadership meetings. This regular review shows the progress of the team and allows everyone to reflect on how on or off track we are with our thinking for each horizon. Not only is it satisfying to see what's been accomplished, but it also creates great team bonding as everyone sees what they thought was impossible twelve months ago and what has happened since. Ninety percent of the time the progress is positive, and the team has achieved much more than expected.

And here is what the finished horizon thinking template looks like:

VISION: Teach the most critical skills to the next generation of technology leaders

Horizon 1	Horizon 2	Horizon 3
• Launch new training class for IT managers • Review feedback and revenue every six weeks • At twelve weeks, business review and decide to keep going, change direction, or pause training	• Launch next level technical skills training to beat competitors • Develop app for on-the-go training • Certification program launched and recognized by leading employers	• Establish an IT leadership summit in person • Attract 250 leading IT leaders to attend, and build it into the most exciting IT event of the year

---

One more note on horizon thinking before I move on. This form of thinking is also an effective tool to use in your personal life, whether you are planning a project for yourself or with other people in your family. For many of us, work and home have become the same physical space. There's no reason why you can't bring work tools and ideas into your home and vice versa.

How to Use Three-horizon Thinking for Innovation Planning

Now we look at using three-horizon thinking for innovation planning. This is a structure that can help you and the team identify both incremental and disruptive innovations that get developed and launched in nonlinear timeframes.

Depending on how developed your vision is, your competitive position, and the changing customers in your industry, you will decide at what pace you innovate your core business and create future new businesses with disruptive innovations.

Below I use a slightly different example than what we've been using above. This is an example of an IT service company that is facing near- and long-term competitive pressure.

VISION STATEMENT: Become the go-to leader in IT business services for the hybrid work world

Horizon 1 Incremental innovation in our core business	Horizon 2 Growth innovation that creates adjacent business	Horizon 3 Disruption innovation that changes our business
• Survey clients on new needs and satisfaction • Competitor service review • Launch update to main services to include work-at-home support	• Acquisition plan for adjacent business services that clients use • Task product development team identifies two adjacent services we can launch organically within twelve months	• Create a team to test generative AI support capabilities • Launch industry's first AI tech support team • Get to market in six months to beat any competitive threat

These horizon options are fast frameworks to use because you are not aiming for perfection; you are aiming to move forward. Perfection is the enemy of becoming unstuck, so throw out that perfection-shit thinking.

THIS WAS A PACKED CHAPTER, and you're now prepped with the new thinking techniques from the best tech companies and leaders in the world and ready to apply them to your business and with your team. Though this is a business book, you can adapt any of these new thinking frameworks for life outside work. You are a whole person, and you need to use your whole self to keep new thinking coming.

TL;DR

- As business continues to shift amid the impact of economic, political, and societal changes, new thinking is now even more of a necessity.

- New thinking tools can make you and your team more purposeful with your thoughts so you can innovate and make progress together.

- New thinking includes associational, critical, concrete, and fantasy thinking, each with their own processes and benefits to finding new and different ideas.

- Using a three-horizon framework can help you add time span and innovation spectrums to advance your business.

4

SHORT-
TERM
TENTATIVE
GOALS

"I wake up every morning and think to myself, 'How far can I push the company forward in the next twenty-four hours?'"
LEAH BUSQUE, founder of TaskRabbit

WHEN I MOVED TO SAN FRANCISCO and started working for a global tech company, I noticed that the chief marketing officer was often with the CEO in a glass-walled boardroom in the middle of the office. I asked my boss about the CMO, and she told me he worked closely with the CEO and the rest of the executive team, developing the direction for the company and making decisions for the future. Then and there I realized I wanted to be in the room where decisions were made and to be part of making them. I didn't want to be on the receiving end of the direction setting; I wanted to be the one setting it. When I researched what I needed to become a CMO, I discovered that many of them had MBAs. And that's how getting an MBA was added to my long-term vision and future version of me.

Now, I had barely scraped through university, even after five years of classes, and I had no SAT score to submit to MBA programs in the US because I had gone to university in Canada. That meant I had to figure out how to get into an MBA program starting from the bottom. Those actions went onto my short-term tentative goals list. Working through the process step by step, I was eventually accepted into the MBA program at Dominican University of California.

When I was halfway through the MBA program, I took off one semester to have our son. That turned into another semester, and eventually I ended up taking three semesters away from the program. By then I was in a full-time marketing job, had two small children, and travelled a lot. I was starting to think it was time to let go of this long-term MBA goal. I had dinner with a successful friend, and she helped me validate the doubt I had. My friend had launched her own business, and it was growing and attracting major brands as clients. She said she had thought about doing an MBA and had even taken a few courses, but she realized she could learn everything she needed by building her business. I held on to that story and felt it might apply to me as well.

When I called my sister Megan to talk it through and get her agreement that I should strike the MBA off my vision list, she said, "Oh, I understand. You don't need to finish the degree." Then she added, "I'll completely support you as long as you feel good about what you'll tell your daughter when she asks why you quit." Well, that was a gut punch. I stammered out an answer and said things like, "Well, it's hard! And I'm tired all the time! You try to handle all this! Do I even *need* an MBA?" Finally, I hung up feeling more frustrated and confused than ever. Was my long-term vision worth it?

As I lay in bed that night, I realized I had no good reason for quitting. I still wanted to be a CMO someday, and I was simply frustrated by all the short-term challenges to meeting my long-term vision. I got on my laptop and logged on to register for a class in the next semester. I was back to short-term tentative goals and on my way to the long-term vision.

———————————

MOST HIGH ACHIEVERS love to set a goal and not just on New Year's Eve. They have a maniacal focus, and if they fall short of the mark, well, holy shit, look out. I was this goal setter, a hard-core, goals-set-in-stone person. And if I missed those goals, I felt like a failure and piled the guilt on myself.

There are many kinds of goal setters: those who have a ten-year outlook, short-term goal setters who are crushing it each quarter, and all those in between. What I've noticed as I talk with lots of people around the world is that most of their goals are fixed, and they either hit them or not.

In today's complex business and social environment, I believe in getting comfortable with the concept of setting short-term *tentative* goals. I introduced this concept in the previous chapter when talking about tentative conclusions. So much can change so quickly that your best bet is to stay open to integrating new information and updating your goals as you go.

This idea of setting short-term tentative goals doesn't detract from progressing toward your vision. Instead, setting short-term tentative goals can work as a magnet for momentum and success as you and your team are on your way to achieving everything you've dreamed of.

Long-Term Vision and Short-Term Tentative Goals

In chapter 2, you started working on your long-term vision for your business and for your future self. Tech leaders have been using long-term vision since the start of the industry and continue to set ambitious goals.

Here are some visions for tech companies we know today but were outrageous in their thinking when they started:

- Jeff Bezos's tagline for Amazon in the early days: "Earth's biggest bookstore."

- Canva's mission: "Empower the whole world to design."

- Google's mission: "Organizing the world's information."

- Uber's early vision: "Transportation as reliable as running water, everywhere for everyone."

- Bill Gates's vision for Microsoft: "A microcomputer on every desk and in every home running Microsoft software."

Bill Gates famously said, "Most people overestimate what they can do in one year and underestimate what they can do in ten years." Looking back at the big visions these innovators set out for their organizations, it's easy to think that success was inevitable, but it was not. All these companies encountered barriers, roadblocks, and near-death experiences on their way to greatness.

Ever read business success stories and wonder how that company raced to the top? Well, in the tech industry, most successful businesses have taken more than ten years, as I mentioned in an earlier chapter, and had leaders with long-term visions and short-term goals. And by working those short-term goals continuously, and using other concepts like new thinking, they kept moving ahead.

One seemingly overnight tech success story that spans a decade is Zoom, the all-in-one intelligent collaboration platform. In 2011, Eric Yuan was working at large tech company Cisco in a comfortable, well-paying job when he made the leap to leave with a group of engineers to start something new. He wanted to create a new video and voice technology that was better than what existed in the market.

Yuan has talked publicly about being unhappy in his role at Cisco and deciding that, even though he had a six-figure salary, he needed to go create his own company. "On the one hand that's indeed a big risk, to go from a very well-paid and vice president position [at Cisco]. Why would you want to leave?" Yuan told CNBC's Make It. "However, on the flip side, I was not happy. So, mentally, that's not a big risk. The purpose of life is to pursue happiness, and I was not happy. Then what's the risk?"

It took Yuan's team two years to build a sellable product, and in 2013 they finally launched the software. The early days were hard for the company, as they had trouble finding investors because the videotelephony market was already crowded with companies. The first round of Zoom's funding was $3 million, which by tech standards at that time was low.

However, even as Yuan led the team to the long-term vision, he used short-term thinking to navigate the daily challenges. He had daily check-ins on his own happiness level, which was important to how he interacted with his team and family. He focused on creating happy customers and building a culture, day by day, that everyone would be proud to work in. These small steps were all critical to long-term success.

Fast-forward to the beginning of the pandemic in 2020. Zoom had already seen success and gone public on the New York Stock Exchange a year earlier. As companies sent employees home, they needed to connect over video, and Zoom became a household name with hundreds of millions of people connecting on the platform every day.

The media stories about Zoom made it sound like the company had achieved huge growth overnight. But in truth, the team had been working for a decade to create and continue innovating its technology. And Yuan didn't forget his long-term vision and quest for happiness; it was central to the company's messaging and values.

Sustaining your long-term vision takes endurance and resilience in the face of many challenges that can come your way. Setting short-term tentative goals can give you the momentum and progress you need to keep going. In using both long-term and short-term thinking, you will need to stay flexible and open to what comes your way, which is why tentative goals can work for you.

Strong Opinions, Loosely Held

Tech leaders stay clear and firm on their vision but open on their short-term goals. Basically, they keep those short-term goals flexible as they navigate the complexities of building a business.

Tech founder and venture capitalist Marc Andreessen uses the phrase "strong opinions, loosely held" to illustrate this. This phrase combines the necessity for a leader to have a clear vision and strong opinions and the fact that new information is always emerging. Smart leaders understand that their ideas and thinking must keep evolving in order to realize their vision.

> If you're going to start a company around that [a strong conviction], if you're going to invest in that, you better have strong conviction because you're making a very big bet of time or money or both. The problem is it's a strong view, great. What happens when the world changes? What happens when something else happens?
>
> And the way the world works kind of in business and investing and other places is just when you think you have everything figured that everything changes. So the sort of system evolves, and things happen. And so what do you do when the world changes?

Let's say you are a business leader who has set your company's vision to be number one in its category by solving your customers' most pressing needs. The company's short-term goal is to launch a new product for the core audience and achieve $5 million in revenue in year one. The company is hell-bent on getting the product out and reaching that goal by end of year.

Your company is successful in getting the product launched and running a marketing campaign, and the sales team is trained with messaging and is out in the marketplace having conversations with prospects. But then feedback arrives that says the product is not meeting the biggest need of the target audience—it's a nice-to-have but not a must-have product. Sales are slow, and you push your sales team harder because you are a leader who meets goals. Those targets were set months ago, and there is no way you are changing them now.

More negative feedback comes in, and now it's pissing you off. You think your team is making excuses for not focusing on the goal. You double down on the pressure with your sales and marketing team. The message goes out that nobody is taking time off until this shit is figured out and you're back on track to meet the goal. You feel like an asshole, and the stress is thick every day. One person resigns and then another one—one you don't want to lose. After months (or years in some situations), you pace the house late at night trying to work out what you're doing wrong, why you're operating in a way that is counter to your values, and eventually you realize that you fucked up.

I've heard variations of this story many times. Stories where leaders become so locked on their goal that they forget their values, make a negative impact on their culture, and lose good people, all in service of their goal. This is wasted energy, power, relationship capital, and it incurs far too much stress. Instead, when you use the tool of tentative goals, you keep your mindset agile as you carry out your vision.

How to Work with Tentative Goals

Let me rewrite the above scenario using tentative goals. You still have the same vision, and you believe you've found a business need the company can meet with a new product, and you launch to the core audience. You still believe you can reach $5 million in revenue this year with the product and set a tentative goal with your team to reach that target. But as the marketing and sales teams prepare to go out, you say, "Let's be curious. Let's see if we can meet that goal or do even better." The launch happens and the team is talking to current clients and prospects. Some sales start to come in. Then comes feedback that the product doesn't solve a priority issue for the client, and sales slow. Now you get curious about assumptions that were made on the audience's primary business issues. You go back and look at the research and partner with sales on a few conversations with prospects to hear more. In one of those meetings, you get an insight that allows you to see how you can change the product to meet one of the most important needs you are hearing about.

The product design team does a mock-up and shows it to a few clients. The feedback is great, and clients place orders. Sales and marketing rework their message and campaign and are feeling energized that they've worked together as a team with you to get this right. The team goes back to market and then starts seeing traction. The team ends the year just behind the tentative goal and celebrates by talking about what they learned and what ambitious goals they can tentatively set for next year.

Now it's possible that the outcome in both scenarios could be the same: the revenue comes in just under the goal of $5 million. But in the second scenario, in which you used tentative goals, the resulting experience and skill building is vastly different. Which business do you want to run and work in?

I covered the fight-or-flight response that's triggered when we are under stress in chapter 1. When people are pressured, stress can escalate and creative thinking and problem-solving runs right out the door. You end up frozen and robotic, checking things off the list to feel like you're moving forward, but really you are not fulfilling the long-term vision. You want a team that is energized and has access to all the creative and innovative parts of their brains to solve challenges. The more you do to create situations that are open to new information and updating direction, the more positive it will be for everyone who works with you. The tech industry knows this, and now you know it, too. Tentative goals take confidence to implement and can transform a team's ability to learn and achieve together. You can have a clear vision and continuously integrate new information to keep moving forward. The tech industry has used that confidence to keep innovating to create the future and you can, too.

Activate Your Communication

No matter how skilled you are as a communicator, you're probably not communicating enough or effectively to truly get your team understanding and owning the vision and tentative short-term goals you have laid out. To get unstuck, you must be able to rally others around your vision, influence them to act, and help them feel ownership as well. Here is your roadmap for becoming a star in this area.

Develop Your Message

Write down your vision and stop riffing off the top of your head. Describe what it is, why it's important, and the impact it will have. You can put this into whatever format you want; just get it out of your head, because no one is a mind reader. No matter how many times you think you've told people the vision and tentative goals, I guarantee they won't remember it unless you consistently repeat it.

Share It with Important People (Then Make Updates)

Once you've written your message down, share it with people who are important in your business. This could be your team, clients, prospects, analysts, industry influencers, partners, or investors. Get their feedback, take away what is helpful and work it into your message, and leave the rest behind. Everyone will have opinions, and the goal here isn't to assimilate everyone's point of view into your messaging, but to get some input and engagement early in the process. Getting input brings new ideas and information, which helps you keep moving forward. Through this collaboration process, you're also developing advocates who will help you in the long run.

Insert Stories and Personal Connections

If you listen to tech leaders talk about their businesses, you'll often hear their origin story, which is the personal look at their history that led to the development of their vision. Stories and personal anecdotes create an emotional bond that helps messaging land. Some leaders want to separate their personal life from their business life, but you can bring your whole self to business without getting too personal or compromising yourself.

Start Using Your Message Everywhere

Once your message has landed, use it everywhere: inside your company, in sales meetings, partner conversations, investor presentations, board reviews, in media interviews, and on analyst calls. You will become a freaking pro at your story because you'll use it everywhere, and so will your team. This will lead to a consistent message for your business, and your target audiences will be clear on your vision and what you stand for.

Use Your Message Consistently, Even When Everyone Has Heard It
Even in the tech industry, leaders get bored of sharing the same vision. They think everyone is sick of hearing them say it, and because they are innovators, they are itching to move on to something new. Although there are a hundred ways to innovate in your business, deviating from your vision isn't one of them. So use the same message until you are sick to death of it—and even after that.

That approach worked well for Tien Tzuo, co-founder and CEO of Zuora, a cloud-based subscription management platform. Tzuo coined the term *subscription economy* early on in his company's founding and went on to create a whole new technology category. After the message for the subscription economy was built out, he used that messaging consistently as he and his co-founders grew the business and eventually took Zuora to an IPO in 2018. He wrote a book called *Subscribed*, created a user conference series with the same name, and was relentless, as was his team, in sticking to that message.

Schedule Communication Regularly
The best way to get purposeful about communicating is to schedule communications updates into your calendar at least one hour per week. And when you think you're communicating enough, I want you to multiply what you're doing by three. Then you'll be in the ballpark of the right amount of communicating. Your communications can be a video to your team or company, which includes your messaging and progress on long-term vision and short-term tentative goals. You can write a blog post for your customers, connecting your vision to their successes; a newsletter aimed at your partners, where you reinforce your joint vision and short-term goals; or a letter to investors on your progress. If you make time for this work, soon you'll be in the category of superstar communicator.

Check Back with Your Team

Have your team present a description of the company and its vision to each other. This can be stressful, but you can make it fun. Ask everyone to present in costume or using the voice of a historic figure. Whatever tactic you use, the idea is to have your team say the messaging out loud to practice and own it. Reward those who are positive examples and reinforce with others. Showcase leaders at company meetings and reference those people in conversations. For those who aren't quite there yet in understanding or executing the company vision, continue to reinforce the importance of a single message and acknowledge their progress.

NOW YOU KNOW HOW to become excellent at communicating your vision and short-term tentative goals. These actions, along with commitment to a consistent message about your vision that inspires you, will help keep you unstuck.

Your Tentative Goals Tracker

Creating your vision and tentative goals is a huge accomplishment, but if you have no way to track your progress, you'll end up relying on your memory and miss an opportunity to keep those goals and vision front and center with your team. There are many models available for tracking goals such as MBO (management by objectives) and EOS (entrepreneurial operating system), but the tech leaders at companies such as LinkedIn, Google, Twitter, Uber, and Microsoft have fallen in love with OKRs. OKR stands for objectives and key results and was pioneered by former Intel CEO Andrew Grove. Then venture capitalist John Doerr wrote *Measure What Matters*, which became the playbook for other tech leaders on how to integrate OKRs in their businesses to accelerate results. These systems—MBO, EOS, OKR—are all similar in that they provide a framework to capture, quantify, and track what's most important to your business. Below is a structure you can use right now to get started tracking your tentative goals.

Input Your Vision

First, find some paper and write down your vision at the top. Your vision is enduring and should remain true for many years into the future.

Input Your Three-Year Outlook

For this step, use as much detail as you can, using a mix of narrative and bullet points. If you created a three-year horizon in chapter 3, you can use that content here.

- Describe what your business and team will look like and achieve in three years. Include the clients you'll work with, the partners you'll have, how many people will be on your team, and what experience you hope to create together.

- List your revenue and profit.

- Set out awards and achievements you'll secure.

- Where does your team work, and how do you interact with each other?

- Describe what it feels like to be working together to reach the vision you have in place.

Break Down Your Three-Year Outlook into Tentative Goals for Year One

Let's say your three-year revenue goal is $10 million, and right now you're at $5 million. Work out what you need to meet in year one to get you on track. Do the same exercise with each part of your three-year outlook. If you decide you want Google to be your customer in three years' time, this first year may be finding ten contacts within Google to introduce your business to. You get my point here. By breaking down each part of your outlook, you create your roadmap to success.

Track Your Tentative Goals

Review progress against your tentative goals with your team every quarter. Capture what you learn and remember, this exercise is about being curious and adjusting as you go on the journey. There is space in the template to restate your tentative goals if they need to be revised. This quarterly iteration of review, reflection, and restatement or recommitment will be energizing and empowering for your team and keep them unstuck.

Keep it Brief

You should be able to keep your annual review to two pages so that it can be shared easily with your team. If you're thinking, *Uhhhh, maybe I'll try this later*, push that thought aside and draft it out now.

SHORT-TERM TENTATIVE GOALS **79**

Vision:

Three-Year Outlook:

Year 1	Tentative Goal 1	Tentative Goal 2	Tentative Goal 3
	•	•	•

Q1 Learning:

Restate or recommit?	Tentative Goal 1:
Restate or recommit?	Tentative Goal 2:
Restate or recommit?	Tentative Goal 3:

Q2 Learning:

Restate or recommit?	Tentative Goal 1:
Restate or recommit?	Tentative Goal 2:
Restate or recommit?	Tentative Goal 3:

Q3 Learning:

Restate or recommit?	Tentative Goal 1:
Restate or recommit?	Tentative Goal 2:
Restate or recommit?	Tentative Goal 3:

Q4 Learning:

Restate or recommit?	Tentative Goal 1:
Restate or recommit?	Tentative Goal 2:
Restate or recommit?	Tentative Goal 3:

Many of you were brought up in the system of hard numbers, hard facts, and hard goals. Well, lessons from the tech industry have shown us that there is another way to operate that will lead to success.

Creating a long-term vision, setting short-term tentative goals, and communicating them relentlessly are hallmarks of modern, unstuck leadership. By taking some of the pressure and stress out of must-achieve hard goals, you can unlock curiosity within yourself and your team. This also allows your mind to be open to feedback that can lead you in a different, and often a more successful, direction.

This is new thinking for ambitious leaders who feel there is only one way forward—their way. The constructs of top-down decision-making are eroding fast, and our new leadership models promote input and collaboration from around our organization. It's not just nice to have; it is imperative that everyone on your team feels they can contribute to the success and forward motion of the company. The competition for talent is not letting up, and leaders who embrace this new co-creation model will see the real business benefits of employee retention, engagement, and a faster path to fulfilling the exciting vision you've set.

Finally, there are many systems like OKR, MBO, and EOS that help you track progress toward goals, and now you have a new one that focuses on tentative goal setting and includes regular review, reflection, restatements, or recommitments.

In the next chapter, I am going to talk about the techniques and tools that tech leaders use to think and act big.

TL;DR

- Long-term vision is the foundation for getting unstuck, and setting short-term tentative goals alongside your vision will keep you in a state of momentum.

- New information will emerge constantly. Setting tentative goals gives you flexibility to change your short-term actions to absorb that new information.

- Effective communication will activate your vision and short-term tentative goals with your team, customers, partners, and investors. Spend more time communicating than you think is necessary.

- Track your tentative goals in a way that supports momentum and doesn't punish your team each quarter. Include time to reflect on whether your tentative goals are still up to date, and either restate or recommit to them.

5

THINK
AND
ACT BIG

"*I realized that staying behind-the-scenes would hold our organization back. No matter how uncomfortable, it was time to be intentional about being more unabashedly visible.*"

JULIE CASTRO ABRAMS, CEO and chair of How Women Lead

THE TECH industry is full of challenger brands and those who want to be challenger brands. These organizations want to defy the usual, take down the established players, and be seen as brash, bold, and dominant. Canva wanted to open access to high-end design tools. Warby Parker wanted to revamp the eyewear industry. Airbnb wanted to disrupt hotel stays.

Once the realm of start-ups, now even large, long-established companies want to be seen as challengers and often talk about disrupting themselves and their businesses before anyone else can. The companies operating as challengers, and their leaders, offer us some important lessons for an UNSTUCK mindset. They are always thinking and acting big.

Take for example, Whitney Wolfe Herd, one of the co-founders of Tinder. When she left the company and filed a sexual harassment lawsuit against them and the parent company, IAC, there was speculation about what would happen next and how she would move forward in her career.

Wolfe Herd went on to create Bumble with a new point of view. She wanted to upend the dating category, and so she launched the company in 2014 with a focus on building a dating site for women that would make them feel comfortable and in control. As the site gained traction—and I mean tens of millions of users kind of traction—Wolfe Herd expanded into the networking space and friendship connections.

In 2016, the company launched Bumble BFF, which connected women looking for platonic friendships. The move to adding friendship connections on a dating app platform doesn't seem like a natural leap, and who would have thought that adults needed a friend-finding service, but Wolfe Herd's big thinking once again challenged the industry.

Bumble kept innovating, and in 2017 launched Bumble Bizz, which aimed to connect professionals to share and learn. I can't say if the company wondered if it could take on getting into professional matchmatching—LinkedIn rules in this category—but they went for it anyway, and that innovation has kept them moving forward. In February 2021, Wolfe Herd took Bumble public, with the stock (BMBL) popping when it opened and ending the day with a market cap of over $8 billion. All this virtual connecting was visionary, and Wolfe Herd continues to challenge Bumble to stay ahead.

Challengers charge full-on into industries with new vision, unique energy, and sometimes with the goal of taking down industry giants. They never stop innovating, and they launch new products, features, and services at a fast pace, as they simultaneously attract talent, partners, and customers.

If you had the choice of being the challenger or being challenged, which would you choose? I'm certain it's the first, especially if you are reading this book. But being a challenger alone doesn't make you an industry leader or keep you unstuck. Industry leaders become known because they have a vision and think big. They also act big to get their vision and message out into the world. Thinking and acting big are concepts that work together, so let me start with the first of these and show you how using your long-term vision to develop thought leadership is at the core of thinking big.

Thinking Big

Who wants to be a thought leader? Almost everyone I've ever met in business has talked about thought leaders—who is one and how to be one, who thinks they are one but really aren't, and on and on. There is a misconception that you can hire a publicist to get you press and that makes you a thought leader. This is not how it works.

My former colleague Noah Cole, who today leads global communications for Siemens Digital Industries Software, always says that to be a thought leader, you must have a thought. Well said, Noah. It all starts with what you have to say on a topic or subject related to the industry you're in or one you want to launch into. You've already started the process of your thinking big leadership platform by working on your company's vision.

Before we get into the details, I'd like you to think about who influences you.

- Who do you watch, read, and listen to? We did some of this work in chapter 2, so refer to the notes you made there.

- Would you consider anyone you follow as thought leaders? Bozoma Saint John, Shellye Archambeau, and Robin Sharma are thought leaders who influence the work I do. I follow them on social channels, read articles they write and are featured in, buy and read their books, and integrate their ideas into my work.

- Who makes it onto your list of leaders you follow? Once you have a few people in mind, think about why they influence you and what they are doing to put them into the category of thought leader in your world.

If we were sitting together, I could scan the list you've made and give you specific observations. Since we're not together, I'll take a guess that what these thought leaders are doing is communicating a big vision, big thinking, and maybe a counter perspective to the norm. They have a leadership perspective, and they are sharing it across many media platforms. You, too, can think big and develop a leadership platform to share your vision.

Your Leadership Topic

Creating a leadership topic is the first step that think-and-act-big leaders in tech take. Creating your topic breaks down into three steps.

1 **Decide what you're going to talk about.** There can be one or multiple topics that you'll take a leadership position on. Use your long-term vision as a starting point to develop a list of topics.

2 **Decide what your unique point of view is on these topics.** You need a unique perspective or message to stand out. Many tech thought leaders have a challenger or contrarian point of view of their industry that makes what they have to say unique.

3 **Prove it.** Develop the proof points you'll use to back up your unique point of view and why you're taking a leadership position on the subject. This can be data from industry reports, insights you've developed, analysis you've synthesized from others, or your own business data.

Most people get stuck on the first or second step. They don't know what they think, or what makes their thinking unique, so they freeze and go back to talking about wanting to be a thought leader instead of doing the work to be one. You can get unstuck here by writing down your answers to the steps and questions I've outlined above. I promise there won't be a test to see if you stick to these topics, so don't hesitate and just get something down. Once you have your unique point of view, your proof points will help you weave together a narrative and defensible information that supports your leadership position. Remember, you can tentatively decide on a leadership topic and your unique point, start using it, and then refine it or change it as you need to.

Acting Big

Tech leaders, thought leaders from all industries, and famous people take specific steps to get themselves noticed, followed, talked about, interviewed, funded, hired, and referred. And they keep repeating activities with new content in new arenas to create momentum in their business and careers. You can act big, whether you are an introvert or an extrovert. It's an essential part of fulfilling your vision and keeping unstuck.

The concept of acting big is a simple one. Broken down into its essential parts, it looks like this: create a vision for the work you're doing, craft your message, and start communicating it. Before we get into the specifics of how you can act big, I want to emphasize that acting big does not make you an ego maniac; it supports your future goals and inspires others to aim for their biggest goals as well. This will become easier once you choose the activities that feel natural to you and start doing them regularly.

For many years, I wouldn't engage in any work that put my perspective, vision, or leadership opinions out into the world. I believed that my hard work, at work, would be recognized and rewarded and I'd create success by keeping my head down and delivering. Seeing how leaders in tech created momentum and success by acting big with their content, on stage, in the media, at industry dinners, and as judges for awards eventually brought me around to the understanding that I needed to put aside any doubts and start acting big. I was often looking for someone like me on stages and in the media, and as more women became more visible in the industry, I wanted to be, too, so that others would join me.

In my network, more female than male executives are uncomfortable with this topic. Some get quiet and withdraw when I start to talk about acting big, and they start to check emails and social media, basically tuning me out. Others say they know people who do this well, but it's just not something they can do or have time to spend on. Still, others protest loudly about why they shouldn't have to do this and that their work should stand on its own.

I also want to acknowledge that there are still many work cultures that won't support anyone but the C-suite acting big. A partner at a big five consulting firm confided that she had started acting big in her specialized industry area and found herself frozen out by some peers after she was quoted in a few published articles. She asked some of her team what was up, and one let her know that they didn't think it was right for her to outshine them with press coverage. At that time, she had to decide if she would continue acting big or if she would step back and wait for a time when it wouldn't make her peers uncomfortable. She went back to her values and started working on how to align with her work or make the decision to exit.

Ten Ways to Act Big

Acting big doesn't have to feel intimidating. There are activities on the following list for everyone, but it's not exhaustive. There are many more ways you could add to the list that will help position you as a leader in your industry, but these are great starting points.

1. Choose a social channel you love and will actually use

What type of social media user are you? Active or lurker, occasionally or never? With this acting big tactic, you don't have to download every app and spend hours each day posting. Pick the one channel you'll use or the one that your industry is active on and begin. You can start by following other leaders, post your own comments, share content, and comment on topics other people share.

Acting big on social media can lead to real business advantages, including attracting top talent, prospects, invitations to prestigious industry organizations, new partnerships, and more lucrative rounds of funding. The UK agency Hard Numbers started an annual report investigating the correlation between a CEO's presence on social media and their ability to fundraise. Its report revealed that unicorn companies (they define unicorns as privately held companies with a valuation of above $1 billion) whose founders have the largest number of LinkedIn followers secured over 20 percent more total investment than the average total raised across the UK's entire unicorn cohort.

Social media posting—seems simple, right? To see a master class in using social media to act big, look at Bozoma Saint John. She is a marketing legend who started in consumer brands and over time has built her career in tech, working in roles at Apple, Uber, and as CMO at Netflix. Her Instagram is active, and she not only shares her life, work, and interests but also cheers on other people, comments on other leaders' posts, and promotes people, companies, and causes she believes in. Marc Andreessen is another tech icon and social media powerhouse whom the entire industry watches to see his forecasts for the next big trend and who he is following and promoting.

2. Meet in person

Going out for a coffee or drink with someone in your network (or meeting over video if meeting in person isn't possible) seems simple, but many of us are unlikely to do this, which is probably due to being locked down in our homes for a few years. Meeting in person whenever possible can lead to stronger connection and different ideas emerging. Yes, it can be hard to leave the house to see someone in person, but starting small with a meeting every few weeks will help you get into the habit of acting big. Also, don't worry that you're bothering someone when you ask to meet. If they are busy, they just won't get back to you. Don't take that personally, and simply ask someone else. I am in the habit of connecting weekly with someone I haven't seen in a while. Sometimes it's a former colleague or someone I went to school with. Other times it's an industry connection or someone I've never met but was introduced to via a contact. To book at least one meeting a week, I reach out to four to six people every few weeks.

3. Create content

Over time, developing content such as 250-word blog posts or three-minute videos will create a body of work that positions you as a leader. You can post links on your social channels back to the content, which creates another great loop.

You may already have your own online platform where you can post your content, such as your company website. If that's not an option, or you want to go bigger in this area, you can talk to partners you do business with and ask if they have websites or email newsletters that you can contribute some content to. LinkedIn is another platform where you can post your thought leadership content. This idea ties in with number six below, because you can create content that you use to pitch a story to a journalist. If they pass, you then have the content ready for other platforms.

4. Volunteer

If you feel shy about attending events but have one on your list you'd like to go to, ask the organization if you can volunteer. This gives you a purpose for being at the event, you get to meet other volunteers—which strengthens your network—and you will get the chance to hear much of the content that is presented. That should give you lots of ideas for social media posts, which will show others in your network that you're part of what's happening.

5. Attend an event and commit to meeting two new people

This move got upended when in-person events were canceled during the pandemic. But online versions of events do provide an opportunity to connect personally, and hybrid events are the future. I know a lot of people who get sweaty thinking about small talk at an event. Take the pressure off and tell yourself you can leave the event after meeting or talking to just two people. That's it, just two.

6. Pitch a byline and interview on your area of expertise

Find out who the journalists are that write for publications your target audience reads. Then devour their coverage so that you learn what kind of reporting and writing they do. Once you have an idea about how they work, you can put together an idea for a story that is a few paragraphs long, tailored to what they write about, and email that to them. Follow up with a call or DM them on social media if they are active. Media are always looking for new stories and appreciate connecting with experts.

You can also sign up to receive email alerts from HARO (HelpAReporter.com), a site that connects journalists with experts in various fields. Once you sign up, you'll receive emails that have lists of specific media requests for stories they are working on now. Another similar resource is Qwoted, a platform that connects media with spokespeople and content creators.

7. Ask to judge an award

Most people don't know that you can ask to do this. I've had lots of success with this one. First, if you belong to an industry association, check to see if they have annual awards. If they do, approach the chair of the association and let them know you'd like to be a judge at the annual awards. Second, identify and write down a list of the media that cover your industry and then see which ones offer awards. Almost all industry media awards use industry leaders to judge them, and they do a lot of promotion of those judges as part of the awards package. Again, you can reach out to the awards contact at the publication and ask how they choose judges. The worst people can say is no, and that's not terrible at all.

8. Enter yourself for an award

Yes, you can enter yourself, and you should. Some awards do need a nomination, but for most you can submit yourself. Depending on your goals, you can use different strategies when applying for awards. One strategy is to be exclusive and aim for your industry's highest awards. Study the winners and what is written about them to understand what you will need to get the award. This approach may take you many years to accomplish, but it may be worth it. Another strategy is to submit yourself for more wide-ranging awards, such as the Stevie Awards, which has many award options and categories.

Submitting yourself for many different awards might be an easier path to winning more quickly.

Winning awards builds your credibility as a leader and helps you to secure speaking opportunities, win other awards, and land media interviews. These are all opportunities that will keep you moving toward your vision.

9. Speak at an event

Lots of people want to try getting on stage but wonder how exactly you get there. Most conferences start securing speakers six to nine months in advance of an event, so begin by creating a short list of events that you'd like to speak at. Visit the promotion pages for the events and look around for information on how to apply to be a speaker. That section will give you the specifics of the topics they want speakers to cover and how to apply.

Once you've applied, don't leave it there. Email the organizer and ask to speak to them about the event and your submission. You can get their feedback on your topic and adjust your submission on the fly. Creating a connection with the organizers will have you top of mind as they make selections.

If you don't have much public-speaking experience, start by pitching industry associations, colleges and universities, and community groups. Reach out to ask if you can speak with their audiences about your leadership topic. You can then use those opportunities to build your speaker resume. Once you have confirmed speaking events, invest time in developing your skills with a trainer or classes. You'll want to capture video of you speaking to use for additional opportunities.

10. Create an event, invite the industry

Creating an industry event is a gigantic leadership move that can immediately put you in a powerhouse position. However, the effort needed to create an event can be enormous, so proceed with caution. To take an initial step toward this, you can put together your own webinar on your thought leadership topic and test it to see how your target audience responds to your content. Another idea is to hold a small, intimate dinner or lunch on your topic and invite industry influencers to attend. By curating a small group, you'll give attendees a chance to get to know each other and discuss an important topic with other leaders.

THESE TEN IDEAS for acting big will take you far and create opportunities you could never imagine today. But there are many more acting big actions you can take and may already be taking. The most important point is that you can start this today as part of being unstuck forever.

Yes, putting your vision out for others to see can be uncomfortable and may even make you feel vulnerable, especially if you were raised in a culture that discourages actions that feel like self-promotion or that may be perceived as bragging. So, let's work through how staying invisible can limit your opportunities and ability to keep unstuck.

Tall Poppies

While I was talking with a group of successful tech leaders at various stages of building their businesses, I started introducing the idea of acting big but quickly sensed hesitation from around the room. Rather than keep going, I called a quick break and decided to check in with a few people to find out if what I was feeling was correct and why this topic wasn't landing with them. Before I got a few steps away from the podium, I was pulled aside by an entrepreneur who asked, "Have you heard of tall poppy syndrome?"

"No," I replied, as I scrambled around in my jet-lagged brain for any reference to that phrase.

"It's the idea that a person who is too successful and stands out gets cut down by others. Get it?" The entrepreneur went on to tell me that the idea of promoting your business and success too much is seen as negative, and that's why the topic of acting big was uncomfortable for the group.

Sharing your point of view, thoughts, and successes are part of the unstuck journey for leaders. But for those under the shadow of tall poppy syndrome, the concept of sharing outside of a small circle you know and trust may be hard to work with. Unfortunately, when you become publicly visible, this can sometimes be mistaken by others as egomania or self-absorption. However, this is the opposite of how to think about acting big.

Though I didn't grow up knowing about tall poppy syndrome, I did grow up in a Canadian family, with an immigrant father, and had all the benefits of a culture that is hardworking, respectful, and modest. Early on in my career, I put my head down and worked hard. I believed that my achievements and efforts would be recognized by others, and rewards would come along with that. I didn't put my opinion or voice front and center; instead I chose to support others by helping in the background. In doing so, I limited my career and kept myself stuck in a specific operating mode that disadvantaged me professionally and financially.

When I moved to the US and started working with global tech companies, I noticed that people gave their opinions freely, promoted their work, objected to others, argued their points, and were insistent when they believed strongly in a position. Generally, they didn't sit back at all. In most meetings, I believed that someone else likely knew better than I did and that I should only talk if I had something different to add to the conversation. This left me behind many times, and embarrassingly, I would get called on by my boss or someone else's boss to ask if I had anything to add. I was deeply insecure and thought my colleagues would always know more than me. As I became accustomed to this US tech work culture, I realized I needed to figure out how to work differently. My first step was to decide that I would present an idea or contribute in some way within the first ten minutes of any meeting. That meant I needed to prepare for every meeting more thoroughly. I needed to develop stronger opinions and work through my discomfort if someone challenged my ideas. By participating early in each meeting, I released my own stress about getting involved, and that allowed me to ease up and contribute more. Because I was preparing more for meetings, I had better constructed reasoning for ideas and reviewed others' past content and contributions and upcoming plans so that I had opinions on how they fit with goals or didn't. I could then ask better questions, make connections, and challenge others in meetings. This preparation and participation positively changed the way people thought of me professionally, and they started to seek out my input and ideas. It was the cornerstone step for me to develop myself and stretch for more challenging roles. As I experienced this change, I started a mantra of "Don't be Canadian" when my nerves crept in. That helped me put myself into the conversation, speak up early, ask an important question, and stand out from my peers.

Changing the Environment

If you find yourself concerned about appearing egocentric or self-absorbed as you share your leadership messages and successes, now is the time to look at how this might be holding you back and limiting your thinking. Perhaps you are shrinking away from the limelight because you believe someone else knows more, knows better, is better educated, or has better experience than you. But if you have a big vision and you are working to get unstuck, you will need to put yourself front and center.

Tall poppy syndrome is a concept that all leaders should understand deeply so that they can spot it and provide opportunity and support to underrepresented leaders who are operating in a business environment that wasn't built for inclusivity and diversity. Changing the ratio of underrepresented leaders is critically important for the advancement of business, government, nonprofits, and academia. There needs to be diversity in making decisions, setting policies, and who is seen as a leader. But you can only do that if you make room for people to share their successes without labeling them a tall poppy or an egomaniac.

When you see the poppies, remind yourself that standing front and center in any room is required if you are going to operate at the top of your profession. For example, if you have a goal to be a leader in your industry and you've recently been accepted to speak at an important event, promote that event and your speaking spot ahead of time. Place it in your company newsletter, post it on LinkedIn, or send a note to clients who may be attending and reach out to other speakers. You'll be talking about important ideas at this event and helping other professionals in your industry. By taking the time to share in advance, you're making sure that your thoughts are getting to those who need them. This is in service of your community and is a powerful way to reframe any nerves you have about sharing what you're accomplishing.

+1 Thinking + Doing

The last idea in this section is one of the most powerful tools for thinking and acting big, and it's a simple one that not enough people use.

+1 thinking + doing is when you take anything you're working on and do it a little bit better. That's it. This one idea will make your career and life bigger and better. Let me show you how this can work.

In my first job out of university, I was working for a tech start-up with very demanding founders. That job was incredible. It was the early days of tech, and we were building the first websites for global brands like BMW and Procter & Gamble as they were trying to figure out what the web was and how to use it. Every day was busy. Even though I was university educated, I barely knew what I was doing. But I showed up, did the work, and felt proud of my contributions.

At my six-month review, my boss, the CEO, sat me down and told me I was failing to meet expectations across all parts of my job. Poor writing, poor organization, poor critical thinking skills, and the list went on. I was devastated and held back my tears through the conversation. He told me that he wanted to work with people in the top 10 percent of their profession. He saw that people made a choice to be top 10 percent or not, and if I wanted to be in the top 10 percent, I'd have to figure it out and work at it. He framed it as a choice for me to make. I could choose to operate in the top 10 percent of my profession and stay or decide that wasn't for me and leave the company. Over the weekend, I thought through the top 10 percent idea, an idea I had never heard of before. On Monday, I told the CEO that I did want to be in the top 10 percent of my profession and needed help to get there. The next day he put thirty days of Tony Robbins CDs on my desk (yes, CDs, it was the late '90s).

For the next month, I listened to a CD each day and then we discussed the ideas. I started to make changes that worked for me. One of the concepts that stuck is that most people do the average amount of work in their job but those who were exceptional usually only do a little bit more to generate outstanding results.

I started to try out new ideas based on that concept. When we signed a new client, instead of filing the contract and letting the account team get on with it, I developed a letter from the CEO that was delivered to the client with a welcome gift full of swag from our company as well as products from some of our premium clients. That welcome gift demonstrated the care we would take with their project and showed that we understood that they were among other leaders in the space. That one extra step in onboarding new clients led to a 20 percent increase in referrals, a huge win for the company. By implementing +1 thinking + doing in the following months, my career took off, and six months later I had a 50 percent pay increase because I was driving so much value for the company.

When was the last time you were surprised and delighted by someone or a company who went a little bit above your expectation?

Recently, a post on LinkedIn caught my attention because it was a beautiful, human example of +1 thinking + doing by a tech company. A friend had lost their dog suddenly, and when they called Chewy, an online retailer of pet food and other pet-related products, to cancel their subscription, the customer service rep listened closely and was empathic. They cried together and talked about their love of animals. The call finished, and my friend decided that they would use Chewy again if they ever got another pet, because of this interaction. Three days later, a beautiful flower delivery showed up on my friend's doorstep. The flowers came from the company and were accompanied by a note from the person who had expressed care and sorrow for my friend's loss. That small action has made my friend a fan for life, and they will refer everyone they ever meet to order from Chewy. +1 thinking + doing = huge impact. You want to get unstuck? Think about the little step you can take to do a bit more and then do it.

Thinking and Acting Big Template

You are so ready to think and act big, so use this template to start drafting your leadership messaging and setting targets for acting big actions for the coming weeks. In the following template, write down three thinking big leadership messages that are important to you. Then move on to write down proof points and monthly targets for acting big.

Thinking big leadership messages	1. 2. 3.
Proof points	1. 2. 3.
Choose a few acting big priorities each month and log them to see your progress and outcomes	Acting big monthly targets
Acting big priorities Take two act big actions each week	1. 2.

Social media posting	1. 2.
Develop content for a blog or website	1. 2.
Meet in person for coffee/drink or video chat	1. 2.
Volunteer	1. 2.
Judge an award	1. 2.
Submit yourself to an award	1. 2.
Pitch a byline or interview to a journalist	1. 2.
Attend an event, meet two people	1. 2.
Speak at an event	1. 2.
Create an event	1. 2.

Thinking and acting big is one of the prominent behaviors of tech leaders. There can be many barriers to overcome when pushing yourself and your team to operate at this level, but I know it's the level you want to be at with your business and life.

Next up, I'm going to tackle the idea of unusual moves that tech leaders use to keep progressing their businesses ahead.

TL;DR

- Find stories of challenger brands and bring them to your team as case studies to discuss.

- Start work on becoming a thought leader by deciding on the topics you want to be known for. Write down your points of view that you can share with others in your network and industry. Are they different from what is out there? Are they relevant?

- Select something from the Ten Ways to Act Big list that feels right for you. Start now and don't overthink it!

- If acting big makes you feel nervous or vulnerable, know that it's a common feeling that you can work through. Practice putting your point of view across in the world and meeting new people. Once you have some success, you'll build confidence and be able to take on more visible opportunities.

- Apply +1 thinking + doing to more of what you're doing now and in the future. +1 means that whatever you're working on, you will improve it little by little each time to create an experience or result that differentiates you from others. Teach this concept to your new hires and to anyone you mentor. It's a life skill for leaders.

6
UNUSUAL
MOVES

"Swipe from the best, then adapt."
TOM PETERS, author and management leader

N IMPORTANT TOOL for getting unstuck is making unusual moves in your business and in your industry. This move is different from taking big bets and risks, which are also important when the time is right. Making an unusual move means taking unexpected steps and doing things differently from how you've done them before, or maybe differently from anyone in your industry. Often unusual moves aren't new inventions but are ideas that are reworked, combined, or presented in new ways. For example, as tech has expanded into every industry, unusual partnerships have also multiplied. Uber created surprise and delight across the US, Canada, Singapore, and Australia when it launched a partnership with the Humane Society that allowed customers to order an Uber that would be shared with puppies or kittens. Not only was the cute factor high for this campaign, there was purpose behind the partnership. All those adorable animals were available for adoption. The campaign also helped the organization raise funds to help animals and raise awareness of animal homelessness. As a result of this positive association with an important nonprofit organization, Uber received a major brand boost from all the global media coverage and social media conversation.

Making an unusual move might mean an unexpected partnership with a company, either someone in your industry or outside your industry, or even working with a competitor.

If you're shocked by the idea of working with a competitor, get ready to read about co-opetition and how working with competitors can work for you. Unusual moves can also mean changing up how you test and launch new products and services, and I will explore that in this chapter as well. All the unusual moves I mention here are widely used across the tech industry. It's up to you to decide which ones you'll implement to keep your business moving forward.

The Value of Unusual Partnerships

Unusual partnerships are exciting to see. They require imagination, relationship-building skills, and perseverance through finalizing decisions to get them to launch. In this instance, when I say partnerships, I mean endorsements, paid partnerships, joint ventures, coalition launches, and offerings that both organizations benefit from when they come together.

The tech industry has made many unusual pairings to surprise, delight, and win the hearts of new and current customers. These partnerships show up with ideas for things you didn't know you needed and that make our lives safer and easier.

As a loyal Chase credit card customer, I see partnerships all the time through offerings from the company. Many of these seem like usual consumer offers, but when you look closer, you realize that there are complex tech integrations behind them that make these partnerships simple to activate.

Peloton and DoorDash have both partnered with Chase and showed up with offers for their credit card clients. Peloton I know well, but DoorDash was not a service I used regularly. When I saw that Chase and Peloton were offering two free months of subscription, I logged in to my Chase account to see more details. The activation was easy: as long as my Chase card was the payment credit card in my Peloton account, I would automatically be credited with two months of the service free. Initially, I was suspicious, because when two companies are involved it's hard to find a smooth and positive experience in which a credit happens automatically. But when I checked back in to my account a month later, the Peloton credit was there. Incredible! And I love both these companies a little more.

With DoorDash, the company's offer was the same as the Peloton one: as long as the Chase card was the payment method for DoorDash deliveries, my annual fee would be waived. I set up the DoorDash app and then connected my Chase card. As you can imagine, my family now uses DoorDash often, and my annual fee was waived as a benefit. The process was simple. There were no calls, emails, or conversations with customer support, because the partner companies worked hard on the backend to make the customer experience seamless.

For all the companies involved in these partnerships, the benefits were multiple. They have acquired a broader prospect base, enhanced their brand experience through the interactions, and no doubt they are sharing data to learn more about their target audiences. These companies offer value for their customers and for their business, a win-win when the partnership is well executed.

Co-opetition

The competition in the tech industry is fierce. Lawsuits, patent infringements, hiring wars, and more transgressions are widespread and well reported in the tech and business media.

Marketing company TechTarget defines co-opetition as "a business strategy that uses insights gained from game theory to understand when it is better for competitors to work together… the goal of co-opetition strategy is to move the competitors away from a zero-sum game, in which winner takes all and losers are empty-handed…The result is profitable for all the competitors when they work together."

Just as the way we work has changed, so has the way we think about competition and collaboration in our industries. For this strategy to work, likely you will need to work on an industry-wide project, or you have a problem to tackle that your competitors are facing as well.

YouTube and Vimeo are both video platforms that are fueled by users loading and sharing content. Although these platforms appear to be competitors, they have found ways to work together that have benefited both companies. In a *Forbes* article, Vimeo CEO Anjali Sud talked about the unusual move to allow Vimeo creators to publish their videos on YouTube: "What it unlocked was actually a totally new strategy for our company… one of the biggest value-adds in our product, and it all came from flipping the script in terms of how you think about whether someone is a competitor or a partner, and prioritizing the problem you want to solve."

Collaborating to Solve Specific Problems across an Industry

The PR Council, led by president Kim Sample, is the only US public relations association dedicated to growth, talent, revenue, profit, and reputation for member agencies and the industry. Its membership includes more than 130 of the country's leading global, midsize, regional, and specialty communications and PR firms. Many of its members compete for clients and talent but find enormous benefits in working together to expand the industry and take on widespread challenges.

The PR Council partnered with Talkwalker to analyze the number of women quoted in US media coverage over a six-month period and found that 32.9 percent of quotes came from women versus 67.1 percent from men. This insight triggered a new program set up by the council. Coined "the Say Gap" by CEO and founder of Man Bites Dog consultancy Claire Mason, the program sought to unite membership in helping to close the gap in women serving as experts to the media and at conferences.

Working with many agency members, the Say Gap program launched with a goal to train 5,000 women as spokespeople. The program included commitment by agencies to provide free media and presentation training to women in business, to spread word of the program by activating social media channels, and to work together to promote more training and encourage more women into media interviews and speaking on stages.

Many of the members competed with each other regularly, but they saw the bigger challenge to solve. They knew that by coming together with a big goal to hit and the expertise to collectively make a difference, they could improve this area of equality for everyone.

Generating Innovative Solutions to Win New Customers

Amazon has powered its way from an online bookstore to hundreds of billions of dollars in revenue and now is in health care, cloud hosting, and other industries. Retailers like Kohl's should've been running scared of Amazon and doing everything they could to distance their products and services and create a clear distinction in their offers. But instead, the leaders of Kohl's decided to collaborate with Amazon, setting up a partnership as a place for Amazon customers to return unwanted packages.

In 2017, Michelle Gass, who at the time was chief merchandising and customer officer at Kohl's (she later became CEO), launched a bold plan to embrace Amazon as a partner. Kohl's and Amazon announced that Amazon customers could return their purchases to their nearest Kohl's stores. At first, I was puzzled, but then I saw the brilliance of this unconventional partnership as it made it easier for Amazon customers to drop off their returns, since they no longer had to go to the post office, which had restricted hours. In return, Kohl's experienced more walk-in traffic from Amazon customers who may not have shopped with them before. It's not hard to figure out that once a customer goes into a Kohl's to return an Amazon purchase, they are probably going to pick up items they need at the same time or will browse and pop back in later now that they are familiar with the store format.

Kohl's and Amazon have created new brand awareness and affinity with their customers because of this partnership. The potential downside of this partnership is if there is any service issue for either company that fails to meet the ease of use for which the brands are known. My husband is an even more loyal fan of both brands now. He buys from Amazon, makes his returns through Kohl's, and then buys more from Kohl's as a result—a win-win all around.

Creating Coalitions to Foster Industry Innovation

As self-driving cars edged onto our streets in the 2010s, tech companies and automakers saw the system-wide understanding and change needed to make them a reality. This new tech demanded new standards, code, safety issues, regulations, education, and planning. Each company had its own agenda and tech roadmap to progress; together they knew they could go faster.

With the launch of the Self-Driving Coalition for Safer Streets, competitors Uber and Lyft joined automakers Ford and Volvo with a mission to educate the public about the societal benefits and safety requirements needed to make self-driving part of the auto experience. More recently, the coalition evolved into an association called the Autonomous Vehicle Industry Association (AVIA), with the original members still involved and new competitors joining. AVIA publishes research by industry analysts and members, lobbies and educates Washington lawmakers, and promotes the latest updates from the government in this area. As an industry-wide team, AVIA advances a mission that has benefits for every company involved.

There are many ways to work with competitors and create more value for your business, your clients, and the industry. The possibilities should feel inspiring to you and help you create new options and opportunities.

Beta Testing and Soft Launches

The tech industry loves a big splashy new product launch. Apple co-founder Steve Jobs became renowned for launching new consumer tech products that were major events in themselves—an unusual move that created mainstream attention never seen before. Tech companies still have big launches, but today they also rely more heavily on beta testing and soft launches to build early connection with their communities, which provide valuable feedback.

When a company is getting ready to launch a new product, service, or offer, sometimes there is a tendency to work behind closed doors to make it perfect. In this scenario, there is a lot of pressure on a team to deliver big on the launch date, and because it is inevitable that challenges come up in the process, an atmosphere of anxiety and stress can develop, which slows down the new thinking needed to work through problems. Too many times I've seen companies use this closed-door perfection approach to finally release their service or product and are then surprised when they receive lackluster feedback. Trying to perfect the product before the launch denies you the valuable feedback that can improve your offer and the chance to make influencers feel included in what you're creating. But using beta testing and soft launches can reduce the pressure and expectation without reducing the vision and goals.

Beta Testing

Beta testing is when you recruit customers and non-customers, influencers, and others in your target audience to test your offer and provide feedback before you make it publicly available for purchase. A *Forbes* Technology Council article details the importance of this step in innovation work: "Focused on the insights of potential users, beta testing is one of the most vital steps in the development of new technology." Beta testing takes place along the journey of development of your product or service. It allows users to experience what you've built but affords you an opportunity to refine some part of the product or service before it becomes GA (generally available), as they say in tech.

You can position the opportunity to be a beta tester as an exclusive early look at your new product or solution. During the process of working with beta testers, you gather critical feedback to see how your new product or service gets used in real life, get validation of features or service aspects you might be concerned about, and increase awareness of exciting new things coming from your company.

Today, even the biggest tech companies run beta testing programs. Google has a Google app beta testing program that anyone can sign up for. Microsoft calls their beta program Microsoft To Do Insider and are always looking for new people to join. Roku and Coursera are other tech companies that are looking to sign up people who are passionate about their products and who want early access to what the company has coming in exchange for their feedback.

If you want to experience this concept firsthand, sign up to be a beta user with a company whose services you use. You'll get insider information about new features and services coming soon. You'll get to meet some of the designers or developers behind the work and ask them questions in community forums or during ask me anything (AMA) sessions. The company will release updates to you to use and ask for feedback, which they'll then take back to the development team.

If you're not already using beta testing in your business, what would it look like to include this as a tactic in your next launch?

Soft Launching

Soft launching is another tactic used by tech innovators. This is when you release your product or service ahead of its official launch data to a small part of your audience, with little to no marketing push. You can think about it as a test run in the real world that allows you to gather more information from a small group and adjust the offer before the official launch date.

A soft launch can be a good strategy to use when you want to get into market fast but still need some runway to make changes. Let's say you are getting ready to launch a new app, and as your team is in development, they have a hard time smoothing the workflow, and there are some glitches to deal with. You get worried because this is an important launch, and the customer experience needs to work.

A soft launch can dramatically lower the pressure to get things right while still working toward the same result. Case in point: during a high-stress, high-stakes product launch, I saw an exchange between a chief marketing officer and chief product officer who were anxious about the live-streamed launch event they were about to have and how the new solution was going to perform. They had created a compelling agenda for the launch that included important industry influencers in studio who were ready to talk about the industry challenges this new solution would solve. Someone walking by the tense exchange said, "Why don't you just soft launch this first so that you're all not so wound up?" The look that crossed their faces was priceless. They realized too late that there was another path that would have given them the same result. Soft launch first, and then hard launch when you're ready.

When you make use of a soft launch, you can still promote your product to your audiences so that they can get access to the offer and give you feedback ahead of the full launch. If you use a soft launch approach, you will still want to set a go-to-market plan for a full launch. But by the time you get there, you will have a better offer and hopefully more confidence in your product solution that's based on input and engagement.

THE BENEFITS OF using beta testing and soft launches are clear. You can set expectations with your audiences that what you're putting out is still open to feedback. Bringing your audience along the journey is an excellent way to build influence and loyalty that can deliver big for you when you're fully live with your new offer. Using beta testing and soft launches can also release pressure from your team in the run-up to going live, because they know changes can be made and expectations will be reasonable. All this testing and input and easing your way into market will keep you unstuck.

Update Like a Cloud Company

In the days before cloud computing (on-demand availability of data storage and computing power), tech companies often released their updates once or twice a year with grand launches on a big stage. The buildup and work to get ready for these updates was all-consuming for their teams. However, once cloud computing was reliable and accessible, tech companies started building their solutions so that they were available on demand via the cloud.

This innovation transformed business models and solutions, including the way tech companies released updates to their products. They moved from a few updates a year that had to be sent to customers via CDs to frequent updates that customers could access immediately on the cloud.

Some companies like Salesforce and Adobe have kept on with the big annual events but now use them more for vision setting, customer engagement, and showcasing the direction of tech solutions. Now almost all tech companies release product updates on a fast schedule, some as often as weekly. These updates may be small, but there can be some unexpected and big updates as well. Have you ever been asked to update an app on your phone? That's the push to get the new features released to users.

If you've been running your product and services updates like an old-school tech company, it's time to update and operate like a cloud company. You might be thinking, *Ugh, more work*, but I bet you do updates to your services and products often already. Now what you need to do is gather those small updates regularly and launch them formally to your clients and talk about them with your prospects.

A McKinsey article on driving growth with product and services launches references a survey that found that more than 25 percent of total revenue and profits come from the launch of new products. Looking for new sources of growth is part of every business strategy, and by launching new products and services, you're building conversation, interest, and attention in what you have to offer from current clients and prospects.

If you're new to the idea of operating like a tech company in terms of your services or product releases, some of the first tools you can use are feature planning and release schedules. With feature planning, you start by looking ahead to what your services and products will look like in either six months or a year.

On a tablet or a piece of paper, draw a horizon with the vision for the new or updated service or product at the far right. Then start to break down that vision into small updates that can be made on the way to that vision. Work with your team to think through which updates can be made by which month and write those into your outline. From the list you've developed, is there a point in time that you can use beta testers to give you feedback? If so, schedule that into your plan.

Here is an example for you: Maria runs a dog-walking service. As more people work between their offices and homes, her business has picked up but is inconsistent. Tuesday through Thursday are the highest revenue days. She's been dreaming about offering a full set of services for dog care—in tech we'd call that dog care as a service (DCaaS). Maria thinks that in twelve to eighteen months, she can expand her services to offer dog bathing, grooming—including nail trims and fur clips—birthday gift packages, trips to the vet, and more. To figure out how she can move toward her long-term vision, she breaks down her short-term tentative goals by looking at the next three months. She decides first to beta test dog bathing services with a small group of clients. If it's successful, in the next three months she will expand that service to all her clients and then beta test a dog birthday gift package that includes a pup-friendly cake, a chew-toy present, and a birthday bandanna. And three months after that, she will release the full dog birthday gift package and extend dog bathing to dog grooming.

By setting quarterly goals for new service releases, Maria can update her clients about future services and keep them excited about working with her. It also helps her create new revenue streams, something tech companies do as they build their businesses.

Ready to Make Some Moves?

Are you ready to make some unusual moves? As you start executing different ideas, you might face hard questions or even skepticism and ridicule from others who haven't seen this in action before. Being clear on your vision and values is your anchor as you try new ideas. Use the following questions to help you work through the unusual moves you're now ready to make.

- Who else do my customers buy from?

- What are some adjacent products and services to my business that combined could make my business a powerhouse?

- Is there an innovation happening across the industry that can be advanced by working with competitors? Is there a competitor that I could create something new with that would benefit both our customers and our companies?

- Can I use beta testing to build relationships with my customers and prospects, ahead of launching my new products and services?

- Is soft launching a way to reduce the pressure of an upcoming new product or service and build buy-in earlier from customers and influencers?

- Is there a wild idea I have for a partnership that could never ever work, and I can't even say it out loud because it's so insane? Write it down here. Then write down what the first step is to make it happen.

MAKING UNUSUAL MOVES is one of the hallmarks of tech companies that are out to change industries, create categories, and take over the world. These companies create partnerships that people thought were impossible or never expected; they collaborate with their biggest, deadliest competitors to develop new solutions that become the foundation of new tech for the next decade; they share customers and come together in unique ways.

Tech companies also make unusual moves when they take their products and services out to market. They know how it's always been done and are open to performing beta testing and using soft launches to get to market before going big with launches that catch everyone's attention.

As tech companies have led the way with cloud and software as a service (SaaS) solutions, they've also changed the expectations on how and when updates are delivered to their products and services. Instead of mega releases of new updates, they set new release schedules in a biweekly or monthly or quarterly cadence. Your customers aren't going to wait long for their DoorDash delivery, and they aren't going to wait long for your latest update. They want it now, please!

TL;DR

- Collaborating with others across your industry can be a powerful way to solve big problems and make progress toward collective goals.

- Unique partnerships with benefits for your customers can come from those outside your industry or from working with competitors. These partnerships can build your brand, customer base, and loyalty.

- Beta testing and soft launching can be added to your unusual business moves to build relationships with your customers, test new ideas, gather information, and take the pressure off new product and services launches.

- Try updating your products and services like a cloud company. More frequent, smaller releases build momentum for your business and excitement from your customers.

7

CREATING
NEW

"The future isn't just a place you'll go. It's a place you will invent."
NANCY DUARTE, principal of Duarte, Inc.

IN THE EARLY '90s, Silicon Valley was a place of unimaginable opportunities and uneasy feelings. While big tech companies dominated and continued to launch new products, people wondered if everything important in tech had been invented. The personal computer was already available, and established software companies were hiring all the talent that Stanford, MIT, and UC Berkeley could produce. For those looking for a new idea, it seemed hard to come by. Then suddenly the internet became mainstream: AOL sent easy instructions for getting online to homes across America and then the world. Suddenly, possibilities were everywhere. The creation of new companies and services increased, and the decade launched hundreds of thousands of dot com companies that were drawing the blueprints for online experiences of the future.

When leaders are stuck, I often hear them wonder if everything of value has already been thought of and created. The answer will always be a resounding no. There are always possibilities for creating new in the world. To do this work, sometimes all you need is the right problem to solve.

Run Headfirst into the Problem

Creating new takes courage and the ability to keep going when nothing is certain but your vision. When you uncover a problem that needs to be solved, you need to be brave to start and persistent and resilient to continue solving it. The problem you find could be one that requires a new process, a new product or service, a new company, or potentially it could even require the creation of a new category of business.

Many leaders in tech talk about having moments of clarity and developing solutions to a problem while they were working on another project. Once they discover what problem they need to solve and create a vision for that journey, they run headfirst into it and continue running, no matter the challenges that come up. Finding a huge problem to solve and running headfirst into it is what led Jasmine Crowe-Houston to the idea for Goodr.

Innovating to Feed the Hungry

Jasmine Crowe-Houston was already an entrepreneur with her business Black Celebrity Giving when she stumbled upon a surprising fact about the immense food waste in the US. At the time, Crowe-Houston was running a pop-up restaurant each Sunday to feed homeless people in Atlanta. As attendance surged at those dinners, she began researching how to get more food donated each week. Through this research, she discovered that the US wastes as much food as is needed to feed every hungry person. As she shared with Guy Raz on the *How I Built This Lab* podcast, "I was blown away with how much food goes to waste in this country, thinking about the millions that are hungry, and thinking wait, we waste all the food that could feed all the hungry. It was just an aha moment and I thought hey, I've got to connect these two."

Crowe-Houston saw the problem as one of logistics: "How do we connect the available food with hungry people?" she asked. Around the same time she was asking this question, food delivery apps were just starting up, and she saw that using logistics and app technology could help solve the problem. She decided to launch Goodr as a tech logistics company.

Crowe-Houston wasn't a coder and didn't have connections in the tech industry. She decided to enter a hackathon at Georgia Tech as a team of one and then started taking advantage of office hours from experts who came by the campus. She developed the wireframes for the website and mapped the logistics of the business as she learned along the way. She created a new business in an area that she didn't have deep experience in or a developed network. But the vision for solving the problems of food going to waste and people going hungry drove her forward. And as her company grew, she realized she was also solving a third problem—the negative climate impact created by food waste. Diverting food from landfills to those who are hungry is part of the value Goodr brings. At the time of writing this book, Crunchbase reports that Goodr has raised over $12 million dollars.

YOU CAN PRACTICE running headfirst into problems by finding solutions to small problems in your business, industry, or community today. Creating new often means you will operate with feelings of uncertainty and unease because you are developing something that has never been done before in your specific way. But you are ready for this journey, because you now have the skills of building a vision, using new thinking, setting tentative goals, thinking and acting big, and activating unusual moves. As you work through your journey of creating new, there will be stumbles and maybe some big falls. But the tech industry is full of those falls and has become known for celebrating them.

Flipping the Script on Failure

The tech industry is full of quotes about failure being the best teacher and the idea that we need to fail on the path to success. The sports world also gives us motivational quotes and stats about how many shots, swings, and baskets get missed, even for the best athletes, on the way to winning it all. I read all of these and have to say that failing still sucks—in all caps now, it really SUCKS! Failure has become built into the operating system of tech, and it's widely believed that failure is fuel for the most successful organizations. The tech industry is full of contrarians and renegades, so it's not surprising that it has flipped failure into a positive. Here are some of the upsides of creating an environment where failure is celebrated, or at least encouraged, on the way to creating new. Much of the upsides are about creating an environment of safety, growth, and speed for you and your team, which will lead to positive business outcomes.

You Fast-Track Learning for You and Your Team

If there is no punishment for trying and failing, your team will feel safe to try anything to move forward. This means better ideas, faster. The fact, there will always be failure on the way to creating something new, so by ensuring your company is a place of safe learning, your team will move faster than other organizations.

You Develop Resilience

While you are learning through the process of trying new things, you'll gain resilience skills and a mindset that acknowledges the fail, finds the learning in it, and then starts again. The pace at which you and your team can come back from a setback creates momentum so that you keep moving forward. You'll want to take time to reflect on what was learned and then lean into action.

You Test Your Vision

Another benefit of failure is that you test your vision. You get real input and data as you work toward your vision, and that input moves you faster toward fulfilling the vision you are set on achieving.

Failure Is Fuel

There are different ways to use failure and the thought of failure to motivate, rather than cripple, yourself and your team as you manage issues and challenges. One approach is to use failure as fuel to create motivation and urgency to see how far your team can go to succeed in a long-shot situation.

Calculated Failure

Shellye Archambeau is a wildly successful leader in tech. She is a board director at Verizon, Okta, and Nordstrom. For fifteen years, she was one of the only Black women CEOs in the industry. Looking at her career wins, including her book *Unapologetically Ambitious*, it's hard to believe that she felt failure close in at times, but it is part of her journey. In the early 2000s, after the dot com bust, hundreds of tech executives across Silicon Valley were searching for new CEO jobs. Archambeau was starting her CEO search with the odds stacked against her. As she told Guy Raz on the *Wisdom from the Top* podcast, she had a weak network in Silicon Valley, a lack of experience as a CEO, no engineering background, and she was a Black woman. Archambeau knew she wasn't going to get opportunities to lead well-known tech companies, so she went after an opportunity with Zaplet, a failing company with an uncertain future. The risk of failure for her was as high as it was for Zaplet. But even though she was warned not to take the role by renowned tech leader Ben Horowitz, she went ahead anyway. She scoped the full range of failure points for the company on the way to landing the role and calculated the outcome to decide if it was the right step for her.

Within a few years, Zaplet merged with MetricStream, and Archambeau continued as CEO. The company was growing fast and gathering momentum, and then "in Q4, 2008, everything just stops," she said, referring to the global financial crash. "We limp into 2009 with very little cash, we've let go of staff, and companies all around us are failing." MetricStream was seemingly on the edge of losing it all. She gathered her leadership team to look at the cold hard facts of the business: the economy was in tatters, sales were plummeting, layoffs were already underway, and more were needed because of the company's dwindling bank balance. "Are we going to fold, or are we going to fight?" she asked the team. Her team could have seen their situation as a failure and given up by deciding to sell or merge with a competitor. Instead, they decided to come out swinging. They calculated the risks and used the thought of failure as fuel to ignite their passion. The company weathered the storm, growing to over 1,000 employees and appearing on the Deloitte Technology Fast 50 list and Red

Herring Top 100. "We acted on our rallying cry of never say die," says Archambeau.

When discussing the risks, Archambeau knew that the road they were taking might lead to failure, so she started by writing down all possible outcomes from the best-case scenario to the worst-case scenario. Then she asked herself, "Can I live with the worst that can happen? Writing it down makes it tangible and if I can live with the outcome I can move forward."

A Common Enemy

Another approach leaders use is to rally a team around a common enemy. Travis Kalanick, one of the founders of Uber, used this approach to defy the old guard and bring in a new way to get around town. As the company started to experience success in San Francisco, it also caught the attention of the San Francisco Municipal Transportation Agency and local taxi owners. Tensions were building between the city and Uber, but Uber ignored the fines and warning letters from the city, which eventually led to a cease-and-desist order arriving at its offices. Kalanick's strategy was simple: the old way of taxis and regulations for ride sharing were the enemy, and Uber would be the knight to slay that dragon and lead everyone to a new transportation future.

Uber created a new category of moving people and have since expanded into food delivery and other services. They effectively rallied their team around the common enemy to create new and move fast.

Failing, reflecting, and then moving forward to trying again is part of being unstuck. As you rally your team to this idea, tell them you want to bring on the failures and the faster, the better. Then, if all else fails, I'll teach you how to quit.

The Pivot Quit

Recently, I was talking with a marketing leader at a Fortune 500 public tech company. This woman was working on a big, long-term goal. She had a great start and was making progress, but as time passed, she lost momentum and was starting to question why she had started the project in the first place. She believed she had two choices at this point: go big and spend more money to keep going or be okay with quitting and accept that it was an idea that didn't need to be completed.

The notion of when to quit is a fascinating one. There are millions of words written about listening to your inner wisdom versus never giving up. You can read all those words and still lose sleep over when it's the right time to quit. And it doesn't help when the results of not quitting are shared constantly in the media. You've probably read a story or two about an entrepreneur who sells everything they own and lives in a hacker house on their quest to bring a new business to life. Down to a few dollars, no money for the next payroll, the last effort to win an important client is the inevitable climax of the narrative, and the entrepreneur eventually gains momentum and riches. Perhaps that is why so many tech industry leaders talk about never giving up. They say that you must be so committed to your idea that even when everyone tells you you're crazy and that it will never happen, you must continue to believe and keep moving forward. So, when do you know when the ultimate move to get unstuck is to quit?

Eric Ries is a Silicon Valley entrepreneur and author of multiple books, including *The Lean Startup*. He is credited with introducing the idea of pivoting as you create new companies and products. In a 2009 blog post, Ries said, "I want to introduce the idea of the pivot, the idea that successful start-ups change directions but stay grounded in what they've learned.

They keep one foot in the past and one foot in a possible future. Over time, this pivoting may lead them far afield from their original vision, but if you look carefully, you'll be able to detect common threads that link each iteration." The tech industry has embraced the pivot as a powerful part of the strategy to move from an uncertain future to success. Tech leaders have reframed their challenges: instead of quitting, they change direction. They keep the vision and keep iterating on their ideas. The act of quitting what you're working on and pivoting to the next winning idea can be powerful and inspiring.

One of the great pivot stories of the last decade is the story of Slack. Now a global tech giant, it was once a gaming start-up with little traction and a floundering team. Stewart Butterfield, co-founder of Slack, initially gained his fame in tech circles for co-founding Flickr with Caterina Fake. After Flickr sold to Yahoo!, Butterfield wanted to build another company and set his sights on creating one called Tiny Speck. He, along with a small group, aimed to build a massive non-combat multiplayer online game.

After many starts and stops, the company realized it wouldn't be able to find success with its gaming company idea, but in the meantime, it had built an internal chat tool that its employees loved. By August 2013, the company had made the pivot to commercialize and release its internal productivity tool and started working toward that as the new business. Eight years later, in July 2021, Slack finalized its sale to Salesforce for $27.7 billion dollars.

What I want you to take away from this story, and the hundreds of other pivots you may read about in the future, is that these could be described as quitting, but instead they are part of a success story. Do you have something you want to quit today? Go back to chapter 3 and see if you could use some of the new thinking tools to take you to a pivot instead.

While you're working hard pivoting to achieve your vision, know that caffeine alone isn't enough to keep you fueled and thinking innovatively. New wellness ideas have flooded into the mainstream, and tech leaders have flocked to them as they continue to create new.

New Wellness

The tech industry tends to operate along a spectrum of extremes, and this is true when it comes to finding the latest wellness trends to support its giant ambitions. People in the industry have experimented with everything from dopamine fasting and micro-dosing to silent retreats and meditation camps. And what starts in tech often gets mainstreamed and picked up by business and lifestyle press, and that then inspires the launch of a new set of start-up companies focused on the wellness concepts they've been using.

There is no scientific or medical report that can quantitatively show the impact of wellness techniques that I am going to talk about here, but that is the point. To get unstuck, you will need to use a wide range of techniques and models. And leaders in the tech industry will try almost anything to gain an advantage when creating new ideas!

Today, the largest venture capitalists in the industry, such as Sequoia Capital and Andreessen Horowitz, regularly gather the CEOs of their portfolio companies for retreats where they immerse themselves in the topics of scaling, talent, and marketing, among others. But one of the biggest benefits for the attending CEOs is the conversation that happens outside of formal sessions. The participants trade work and life information, and it's here where the talk of innovative new wellness techniques is shared. In the 1980s, it might have been cocaine that fueled the finance industry to outperform, but in the 2020s, the wellness trends of energy generation and optimizing personal growth to outperform competitors is part of the tech ecosystem.

So, let's look at a few of these wellness concepts that you might want to consider.

Meditation and Mindfulness

These techniques were embraced early by people in tech. In 2010, Soren Gordhamer developed an event called Wisdom 2.0 that represented the convergence of tech and mindfulness and drew thousands of tech leaders as attendees. Jack Dorsey, former CEO of Twitter and current CEO of Stripe, openly shares his use of meditation, transcendence, fasting and other modalities, which is widely covered in the media—and he's not alone. Marc Benioff, CEO of Salesforce, is also an open supporter of mindfulness and meditation and has even built "mindfulness zones" in half his offices around the world.

Astrology

Seeking guidance from the stars and movement of planets, coupled with hard business skills, is one part of my wellness system. Astrology is an age-old concept that the tech industry first used quietly, then talked about tentatively, and then invested millions in to make it mainstream. A *Harper's Bazaar* article on how millennials and Gen Z have turned astrology into a billion-dollar industry reports, "Terms such as birth chart, rising sign and planetary transits are no longer relegated to the fringes of society; they've taken center stage in our social media feeds, our friendships and, increasingly, the economy. The mystical services market, which includes astrology, mediumship, tarot, and palm readings, is estimated to be worth US$2.2 billion globally." The story goes on to say that "Sixty-two per cent of Gen Z and 63 per cent of millennials say their zodiac sign accurately represents their personality traits, with many also leveraging astrology to help make life decisions—from dating to career direction and even finances, including property and investments." With astrology, there is something that can't be fully explained and that gives my brain some relief from the hard and unrelenting realities of the world.

Crystals

Have you ever noticed yourself being completely drawn to someone rocking a set of beautiful gem bracelets or a necklace, charm, or pendent? Or you're watching a video of someone and notice a giant sparkling gem or a towering spiral of black onyx or pink graphite in their background? When you see that, you may be in the presence of someone who is tapping into the power of crystals.

A few years ago, when I was attending a weekend retreat for tech leaders, I met a high-performance coach for rising executives. This woman was dead serious about her work and up-to-date on every model, system, and case study of the best tech leaders. She was all business when it came to her clients. We sat at the same table at lunch, and I noticed she had a wrist full of bracelets of different crystals. I asked her about them, and she took them off one by one. The obsidian was a protection against any negative energy that she might encounter during the day. It was a big presentation day for her, and she didn't want negative energy entering her mind. The tiger's eye bracelet was for motivation and power, accelerating and helping rid her mind of anxiety and self-doubt. Sapphire was for wisdom, so that she could bring forward all the wisdom of her work to the attendees. Moonstone rounded out her jewels, and she said it represented inner growth and strength. My jaw was almost on the floor as she talked through each one. I didn't expect this expert coach to be using crystals as part of her business routine. As soon as I got home, I started reading more about crystals and asking my friends in tech about who was into them and what their experiences have been. Reports back included increased focus, feelings of extra support, and energy and confidence boosts.

In finding ways to incorporate wellness into your life, using crystals is a starter path to experimenting with fusing your physical space with spirituality.

Biohacking

Hacking is a part of tech culture, so it's no surprise that the idea has made the leap from tech into our biology and wellness trends. Rumored to have made its way into San Francisco tech communities around 2005, biohacking is a broad concept that spans medical and health changes to improve health and longevity. Biohacking operates over a range of activities, with some hardcore hackers trying to edit their own genes, moderates who remove dopamine triggers from their environment, and those who experiment with their diet, stimulus, and exercise.

Extreme athlete Wim Hof, also known as the "Ice Man" for his use and advocacy of extreme cold therapy, has helped advance this biohacking method in the tech industry and now into the mainstream. In a CNBC article on how tech elites are using ice baths to gain advantages with their work, reporter Christina Farr details a day in the life of an entrepreneur running three start-ups who starts each day with a coffee, a run, and then ice-cold showers that help him push through eighteen-hour work days without burning out. Farr calls this entrepreneur "part of the positive stress movement consisting of tech workers who claim that such radical tactics will help them live better and longer or—in Silicon Valley—work better for longer."

When hacking anything, you have some data to start with and then gather additional data as changes are implemented. In the competitive tech space, there are always ongoing discussions of how you can gain advantage, improve wellness for performance, and create environments (internal and external) that lead to new insights and breakthroughs. As a result, new products and services are created and launched to help us understand our bodies better and provide us with data on our sleep, breathing, steps, and exercise exertion. Today, you can use the Oura Ring for sleep tracking, Headspace or Calm apps for meditation, smart watches or phones as step counters or heart rate monitors, and a ChiliPad to regulate your bed temperature. All these products create data that tells us more about ourselves, which we can use to improve our wellness.

HUMANS WILL CONTINUE to create new by finding problems, testing and learning, failing and pivoting, and challenging ourselves to keep going. If you ever wonder if everything interesting has already been done, just think back to the story I opened this chapter with. Just as Silicon Valley was feeling that everything good had been created, along came the internet, which launched the next wave of new. As I write this today, AI is dominating every business conversation with discussions of how this technology will impact work. There is no doubt that unlimited waves of new ideas and thinking are ahead.

In the final chapter of the UNSTUCK model, we're finishing strong with details on how to keep going by spotting behaviors that don't match your intentions; celebrating the big, the small, and all the lessons along the way; and showing you how open sourcing your journey builds even more momentum.

TL;DR

- Find the big problems and run headfirst into solving them. The process of finding and working on the solution for the right problem will be energizing.

- Flip the script on failure. Failure can be fuel, and its benefits of learning, resilience, and mindset are positive outcomes. You can reframe any challenges you have into positives to keep yourself going forward.

- Use the tech tool of pivoting to keep going when you want to quit. Identify where you are having success and spend more time developing that part of your business.

- Tech leaders use new wellness techniques to support their ambitious and world-changing vision. When you are creating new ideas, these techniques can open your mind to possibilities you didn't see before.

8

KEEP
GOING

"I firmly believe that to be a successful entrepreneur you have to fully commit to simply never giving up. Failure only really arrives when you stop trying."

JACLYN BAUMGARTEN, founder of Boatsetter

J ACLYN BAUMGARTEN founded Boatsetter in Silicon Valley when she spotted an opportunity to connect boat owners with people who wanted to have an on-the-water experience. Early in the journey to build her company, she invested significant time in working with an influential manufacturer who was going to come in as an investor and connect Boatsetter to their customer base. It was the win she needed to keep momentum in the business. As she told *Authority Magazine*, a last-minute upset almost cost her everything. "At the last moment, shortly before signing [the contract] and as our remaining bank balance was getting perilously low, a competitor swooped in, and through a relationship with a board member, snatched up that partnership and funding. I felt defeated, and one of my advisers even recommended folding." She could have let this development ruin her vision but instead she made a choice to keep moving. "Two years later, I acquired that competitor, and I now have the relationship with that manufacturer."

As you move toward fulfilling your vision and meeting your short-term tentative goals, there will be new information, roadblocks, competitors, economic changes, and many more unforeseen issues that come your way. Some days, moving forward might mean acknowledging that your own behaviors are thwarting your progress. Or it could mean stopping to celebrate the small and big wins. The best days can be when you stop to share what is working for you and encourage others to build on the success you've started to see.

I will start first with the behaviors and emotions that may surface as you near success, and even as you achieve it, because sometimes you can trip yourself up in the process of getting unstuck.

Watch for Self-Sabotage

You know that feeling in your stomach that is something like nervous anticipation as you make progress on your vision and goals? That's the "Am I really doing this?" feeling I get as I get closer to achieving big goals.

The first time I felt this deeply was during the last class of my MBA. I had spent ten years working toward this goal and almost quit once. Ultimately, I kept going, but when I got to the last class, I was full of emotion about whether I was really going to achieve this goal, which was so close now. During the final leg of this journey, I had to overcome self-sabotaging behaviors and doubtful thinking, as well as strong emotions.

Have you ever felt yourself pulling back as you get close to reaching success? You've spent so long working toward your vision and goal, and you might wonder what happens next. This thinking can lead you to drag your feet as you head toward the finish line. More doubt can creep in, and you might even find yourself delaying the final stages of work with indecisiveness or disorganization. When you do things that counter what you are trying to achieve, this is self-sabotage. Self-sabotage keeps you stuck and is your brain's way of protecting you from fear, failure, and harm. When you start to act in ways that set you back, you'll likely feel confused, and some people misinterpret this as a sign that they shouldn't keep going. For me, this showed up as spending days watching bad TV instead of working on important school projects while trying to explain to myself that it didn't matter if I did well on my final assignments.

Along with self-sabotage, perfectionist tendencies are also likely to emerge for leaders during this endgame. Leaders will think they can't move forward without all the information, the perfect solution, or every little detail figured out. This can be a paralyzing time because your brain fixates on the idea that failure is certain if perfection isn't achieved. That puts you into an all-or-nothing scenario where there can be no winning, but a lot of anxiety and stress. "Perfection is the enemy of progress" is a famous quote by Winston Churchill, former British prime minister, and this is true now still.

When you understand and accept that experiencing new, confusing, and even strange feelings is a normal part of the path to success, you have a better chance of overcoming the thinking and behaviors that don't serve you.

Look at this as a four-part process:

1 Look back at times you've been close to achieving success. Did you experience any counterproductive thoughts or changes to how you were working toward success? If so, what did you think, how did you feel, and what was the impact on you during that time? I recommend writing down your reflections to help you pinpoint what to expect in the future.

2 Check in with yourself regularly and be honest about what emotions and behaviors might be creeping in to stall your progress. When you can identify those emotions, thoughts, and behaviors quickly, that early warning system will help you stay unstuck.

3 If you realize that you are self-sabotaging or using perfection to force a slowdown, use the skills you've learned through this book to circumvent it. For example, review your future you and focus on why this vision and the goals you have are so important. List the successes you've already achieved.

4 Finally, it's important that you acknowledge the fear, worry, and stress you feel. You can feel scared and keep going. You can make tentative decisions and take next steps. You can manage the unknown and remain unstuck. Accept this stage as a part of the journey, and get back to taking action.

Many of us think of success as something to be acknowledged only when we've completed 100 percent of the steps and the outcome meets all our expectations. For years, I was grinding away at meeting my goals and working toward my big vision, thinking that I'd wait to celebrate until the end. That approach robbed me of the joy of the journey and the progress I was making along the way. To stay unstuck, I had to learn to celebrate every small and big success.

Don't Wait to Celebrate

Over the years, my friend and badass businesswoman Barbara Bates has reminded me many times about celebrating successes. In the first year I worked for Barb at Eastwick, we were shortlisted for several important industry awards. I was happy we were shortlisted, but the competition was tough. I was focused on the night of the ceremonies and already feeling pre-event anxiety as I imagined waiting in the audience to hear the award winners. But Barb was all over our marketing team to promote our shortlist status. I questioned her hard about why. Shouldn't we just wait until we know the outcome of each award?

"We celebrate all the successes, and this is a success," she told me. "We celebrate the small stuff and the big stuff." She also told me that if we didn't get the big prize, the moment of success from being included on the shortlist would be gone and our team would focus only on the outcome when there was so much more to celebrate. Point taken.

Years later, I adapted that thinking into the idea of celebrating the wins for as long as possible. One January, one of my teams won a big "company of the year" award, but by February, we had stopped talking and posting about it. Because it was recognition for the entire year, we decided we needed to celebrate it for the full twelve months. We used that award in quarterly business reviews with clients to remind them that they were working with the company of the year. We put it in new business presentations. We updated all our recruiting materials with that info, and we added it to our email signatures and more. I had learned from Barb and found many ways to keep celebrating that win.

Using this technique doesn't only lead to feeling good in the moment; it has a substantial impact on how your team experiences their work. In a *Harvard Business Review* article called "The Power of Small Wins," the authors followed knowledge workers who kept logs of their workdays and noted whether each day was a best day, a good day, or a bad day: "When we compared our research participants' best and worst days (based on their overall mood, specific emotions, and motivation levels), we found that the most common event triggering a 'best day' was any progress in the work by the individual or the team."

Celebrating with kind and encouraging words and acknowledging the importance of all wins, big and small, increases intrinsic motivation and a positive perception of work. And that can lead to a team that is willing to continue working toward the company vision, because they are making progress together all along the way.

Even When You Lose, You Win

In the previous chapter, I talked about how failure can be your fuel as you work on creating new. But even when you believe there is failure in traditional business terms, you don't have to strictly perceive it as failure—just as Stewart Butterfield proved when he pivoted to create Slack.

I worked in one team where our short-term goals included winning new business from large global tech companies. Our first successes were getting invited to conversations and pitches with these companies, and we celebrated those happily. But then when we failed to win any of the work with them, we felt devastated.

After a few big losses, one of the team members, Lindsay Riddell—who is now SVP Global Corporate Communications at Forge Global—came to a meeting with a big thought that changed our perspective about our defeats. "We have to do it bad first. First times are always bad, and that's the only way you get better." I nodded; I could get on board with that. But then she said, "I've also been thinking that even when we lose, we win."

I told her that sounded like bullshit, and she needed to explain. She listed all the ways we were winning and succeeding even though we didn't get the client.

- We were invited to pitch to the companies, and they had been on our dream list (winning).
- We were learning how to present against larger competitors (winning).
- Our reputation was improving, and we had new candidates interviewing with us because they heard we were a team on the up (winning).

By the end of her talk, Lindsay had convinced me and the team. I could see how we were still doing a lot of winning, even when it felt like losing. So it became a norm to find the winning aspect in what we were doing and then celebrating it big time.

Beth Comstock, former CMO at General Electric, is another leader who find the wins in the failures. In her book, *Imagine It Forward*, she explains how she turned failure into success and celebration at GE by launching an event called Failcon. She created the event to help develop a culture of try, fail, learn, celebrate what you learned, try again, fail again, learn, celebrate, try again, succeed, and so on. The event showcased the failures of the marketing teams, but they also highlighted the learnings in those failures that could be used in future work. Those lessons were the successes and a reason to celebrate.

Imagine if every work culture celebrated the success in what was learned and applied. From extensive research undertaken through Google's Project Aristotle, we know that psychological safety is the most important indicator of success for teams. If people feel safe, they will succeed.

Create a Celebration Culture

My team once hit an important project milestone and came into our meeting excited and chatty. When they shared the win with me, I was dismissive, moving right to asking them how they were tracking to the next win. A few weeks later, one of them had the courage to address it with me, letting me know how I made them feel, as if the progress didn't count and there wasn't any joy in moving forward. That was a turning point for me, understanding that recognition and celebration are part of the energy field I can create within my team.

Not everyone feels the need to stop and recognize successes along the way, and many high achievers I know want to wait until all the goals are met to celebrate. I encourage you instead to think about what your team needs if celebrating doesn't come naturally to you.

So, let's narrow in on the culture of your company, organization, or team and have a look at the idea of celebrating along the way, whether it's a win, a lesson from failure, or a success in achieving the big vision and goals. You can start creating opportunities today, or if you already have a culture of celebrating, you can enhance it. No matter what your role in your organization is, from individual contributor to the boss, you have control over what celebrating success can look like.

Here are some ways to encourage your team to share (celebrate!) their work:

- Ask if your colleagues will get together once a month to share case studies or stories of their recent work. Host the session at lunch to include as many people as possible.

- Ask about what worked and didn't work on their projects.

- For things that didn't work, ask what was learned from it so that everyone can use some of those lessons for projects they're working on. One group I know asks everyone to include a section on "What I wish I knew then" to help everyone find the learnings.

- When you meet again, ask for input on lessons learned from earlier presenters that are worked into current projects. Ask about what's happened as they've integrated new learnings.

- Acknowledge everyone who is sharing what they learned and those who are integrating those lessons.

- See if your team is open to having a best-lesson-learned prize each month.

These ideas are a guide, so make this your own and see what works for your team.

If the idea of celebrating along the way is new to you, start small—ask others on your team to help you identify opportunities for celebrating. Here are some questions you can ask yourself and your team to find out where you score on the celebrate-o-meter.

Questions to Ask Yourself

- How good am I at celebrating small and big successes on a scale of 1 (the worst) to 10 (the best)?

- Where do I want to be on the scale?

- What could the benefits be to me and my team by regularly celebrating successes?

- What is one recent mini success that I can take the time to celebrate?

- How do I usually recognize the progress I'm making?

- What are new ideas I can incorporate for celebrating?

Questions to Ask Your Team

- How good are we at celebrating small and big successes on a scale of 1 (the worst) to 10 (the best)?

- Where do we want to be as a team on the scale?

- What are the ways we celebrate today?

- What benefits can come from more celebration?

- How can we incorporate more celebration and recognition with our wider team?

- What are new ideas we can try out over the next quarter?

Open Source Your Success Model

Interestingly, even in the ultra-competitive tech industry, sharing and collaborating for the advancement of everyone play an important role. That's where open source comes in.

Open source is widely used in the tech industry, including at companies such as Meta, Red Hat, and GitLab. These companies make their software or tech available, with the source code, and encourage users to modify or customize it, and then share that with others in the community. Google is a leader in the open source community and promotes its open source technology on Google's Open Source site, where it has Android, Chromium (the web browser that Google Chrome is built on), and many other technologies available to access and build on. By making source technology available for others to use, share, and build on, Google is supporting the global use of the technology, which builds its reputation and leadership position.

The idea of creating and openly sharing ideas, standards, code, and technology approaches can be used as part of keeping you unstuck. Using your experience and leadership role to make models and frameworks available helps others in your ecosystem improve and advance. In return, they contribute to improving the source models and frameworks, and that contributes to building more innovation and connection, moving everyone ahead.

There may be aspects of your business that are ready for open source. One you can practice now is sharing how you innovate, build, and create success in your industry. You can write or record and publish your journey toward your long-term vision and goals. Share with others what's working for you or not working for you. Include specific tools you're using or have created. Invite others to add their own stories of success and build on your ideas to create new ideas that help other accelerate. Some of the benefits of open sourcing your success are:

- You position yourself as an industry leader because you are setting an agenda and convening the conversation.

- You attract talent and new prospects to your company. Leaders want to work for leaders, and prospects want to work with ambitious companies. So when you're making bold moves, like open sourcing your models, you get noticed.

- You build stronger connections with clients by introducing the open source concept to them as part of the work to create more value for the solutions you're offering.

- You meet influencers, media, and partners who want to understand the trends that you're seeing.

When I talk with leaders about using the open source concept, the concern I hear the most is that competitors may get insight into your company strategy, or that proprietary ideas could get shared by mistake and market advantage will be lost. You will need to use your judgment and ask yourself important questions such as: What are the ideas that when used widely create advantage for developing an entire industry? What are the common challenges that face my industry? If you tackled these challenges with others, would that make a huge change for everyone? If there is an answer to that question, that is the time to explore using the open source concept.

Tech venture capitalist Bill Gurley, whom I mentioned earlier, often discusses the benefits and value of open source models, especially for solving complicated industry challenges. "Open source is way better at complex problems than simple problems," he said. In that discussion, he went on to detail stories of how companies like Meta have the Open Compute Project and how Google decided to create Android as an open source technology so that it would be trusted by everyone.

Using the concept of open source in your business is an advanced strategy, but you can start by simply sharing some aspect of your success and inviting others to build on your ideas. Whenever you encourage others to add to your ideas and get into conversation on topics important to them, you keep moving forward.

Show Up, Even When You Don't Feel Like It

There is a misconception that we have to wait for motivation to get up and get going, but the opposite is true. The truth is, you must get up and get going *before* you feel like it, to create your own motivation. I used to often hope for some motivation to show up for me, but instead I started using the technique of reframing to help me move forward. Reframing is when you change the viewpoint of a thought or situation. For example, when I start to get overwhelmed and feel like something is hard, I think about Glennon Doyle's podcast *We Can Do Hard Things*. I say to myself, *Yes, this is hard, but I do hard things*. This reframes my perspective and helps keep me moving.

Here are some other common thoughts and ideas to reframe to keep you moving forward:

- No one will buy my product/service. → The right customer is out there for me.

- I will never be successful. → Success is in moving forward.

- This scares the shit out of me. → I'm scared and doing it anyway.

- I've never done this before. → I can learn new things by just starting.

- No one is interested in what I have to say. → The message I have to share will help a lot of people.

- I'm not sure I can get through this. → I've been through harder times and survived; I can do this.

Showing up for your vision and the version of future you means you are living your best unstuckable life. Business coach and motivational speaker Corinne Crabtree says, "You don't have to want to do it; you just have to do it because you have a future vision of yourself that is more powerful than what you're feeling in this moment."

Feeling stuck might simply last for a few days, but that can turn into weeks, and suddenly you don't know what matters to you or why. And that's when you need this model the most. Because what's the alternative? Do you want to coast through your days? Come on, I know you. That's not how you roll. So, do the work even when you don't feel like it. To keep going, you've got to keep going!

TL;DR

- As you reach your goals, your behaviors and actions may be at odds with your long-term vision and short-term goals. Confusing and strange feelings are normal.

- Learn to recognize self-sabotage and acknowledge your emotions without letting them stop you from moving ahead.

- Don't wait to celebrate. Celebrating small successes (and even what you have learned from the failures) along the journey can create joy and momentum for you and your team.

- Take inspiration from the tech industry's use of open sourcing and share parts of your business or the journey toward achieving your vision. You'll help others and keep momentum.

- You are finished waiting for motivation to strike you. Action creates more action.

9

UNSTUCK

"The view you adopt for yourself profoundly affects the way you lead your life."

SATYA NADELLA, chairman and CEO of Microsoft

YOU ARE now in a position of power with your life, your work, and your thoughts. The tools to keep you unstuckable are in your hands, and I hope you made notes, highlighted sections, turned down pages, and refer to this again and again, because this I know for sure: life is a series of ups and downs, challenges, opportunities, and roadblocks.

In the last chapter, I told you about one of my best mentors and friends Barbara Bates and the infinite source of wisdom that she is. She always tells me not to get too high on the highs or too lows on the lows. I still haven't fully mastered this approach, but it does help me weather the low points and puts the big wins in perspective.

No matter what stage of business or life you're in, at some point you'll achieve the vision you set out for yourself and start to look around for what's next or what's new. That drive to level up is inevitable as a leader, but it doesn't always happen when you expect it to.

Charge or Recharge?

Part of why I love the tech industry and have spent my career working in it is because there is always a next level to develop and explore. The idea of being finished just doesn't exist, and as a result, the culture is one of optimism and progress and limitlessness. Even as I finish writing this book, AI innovations are dominating conversations, and investments in the clean energy sector are ramping up, requiring talent and passion to commercialize the new ideas. Leveling up for you may come after you've achieved a series of goals and you feel motivated to lay out the next set. At other times, leveling up comes after a much-needed break to help you recharge and re-energize. But occasionally you may find yourself in a spot where you can't imagine how you'll ever be able to level up again.

When my mom was in the final stages of cancer and I was traveling back and forth to eastern Canada to see her, I talked to my boss about when I would be working and not working. I held myself together through that time, but I realized that the hardest part would come after my mother died. I told my boss that I was worried about the year after my mom was gone. I needed to grieve and be there for my family, and I wasn't sure that I could work at the high level that my job required during that period.

Five months after my mother died, COVID sent us all into lockdown, which was both terrible for figuring out how to move forward but also helpful because I had to stay put with my husband and kids and work through my grief without all the travel I normally did. It took over a year after my mom died to start to think about my long-term vision and ambition again. For much of that time, I thought that I would never feel inspired or happy again. Few things mattered to me during that period, except for my family, my friends, and my community.

Deep into the pandemic lockdown, I did video check-in calls with several tech CEOs—all men with families who were managing complex businesses through a pandemic and social unrest. Three of them told me they were writing their first books, and I was genuinely shocked. Not shocked because a CEO would write a book—I've worked with CEOs who have written books—but that they were doing it during such an uncertain time in business with so many new demands. I asked each of them why they were making their books a priority and how they were getting them written and published. All of them were getting help. One hired a hybrid publishing firm, one had a full-time writer and editor to work on the book, and another had his marketing team in charge of the book project.

I had had a book on my mind for a few years but had limited my thinking about it being possible. Hearing those stories showed me what a next level could look like for me. I had no idea how to write or publish a book, but I thought there was probably a group of other businesswomen in the same situation. So, I reached out to my network to see who wanted to get together and figure it out. A group was assembled. We called ourselves "The 10," and we got to work. I am so thankful for those meetings and the women of The 10 because it brought back my imagination, ambition, and energy.

Leveling up can also take time. In her book *The Long Game*, Dorie Clark suggests that you look at a decade as a range in which to think about your big level ups. She tells a story about going to see a Broadway show that she wasn't really interested in. When it was over, she burst out of the theater with a new mission—she had to write a script that would turn into a Broadway show. So, in 2016 she set a ten-year goal to have a Broadway show by 2026. During her journey, she's experiencing many ups and downs and doesn't know if she'll make the goal by 2026. But in the process, she's having many experiences and benefits come her way.

What Is Your Next?

Now it is time for you to reflect on what leveling up might look for you. Here are some questions to consider:

- Do you feel there is a next level for you in your life?
- Do you know what the next level looks like?
- Is there someone who inspires you with the level they are operating on?
- If you answered yes to the last question, what is it about that person's life that inspires you and that you want to add to your level up?
- What is one action you can take today toward understanding or moving toward your next level?

When I work on leveling up, I use the tools from the UNSTUCK model, starting back with my values and how I'm living those each day. I revisit my long-term vision and decide if it's time for an update or an overhaul. Through the entire UNSTUCK process, finding inspiration helps propel you forward.

Reading the stories of leaders in tech and business is always inspiring to me. These stories are full of ideas and thinking that help keep me moving forward. Earlier I mentioned the social media prowess of Bozoma Saint John, one of the most successful marketing leaders in tech. I started following Saint John early in her career and watched her moves from Apple to Uber to Endeavor to Netflix. Every time I read about her success, I cheered like she was one of my best friends. Saint John not only shares the good stuff going on for her—and there is a lot of good stuff—she also shares what is hard for her and the truth about her career moves and her life. Her book, *The Urgent Life*, is the real story of her journey, and it has inspired me with new ideas, helped me reframe what I'm working through, and showed me that everyone has ups and downs.

I'm frequently asked if I will ever be satisfied with my business results or how my team is developing: the answer is always no. The world is always changing, so we always need to be changing, stretching, trying, and testing new ideas and ourselves. This doesn't mean that I don't appreciate or celebrate how far I've come. It just means that there is always a next vision to fulfill.

Never Be Stuck Again

We are now at the end, or the beginning is how I like to see it. It has been exciting to share the UNSTUCK model, and now you have access to skills that you can use whenever the stickiness of life and business is getting you down. This UNSTUCK model will carry you through most any situation you find yourself in.

Though you're at the end of my book, your work continues, because business changes keep coming, challenges never stay the same, and all of us are contemplating our next move in an uncertain world. Before the final words, let's take some time to roll the word *unstuck* around in your head and let it provide relief, hope, and vision so you can approach any issue with confidence. There is no getting stuck now: there is always a way forward. It may not be the way you originally envisioned but there is a way, and you will find it, on purpose. In these last words, I want you to feel that whatever you're striving for will happen. Close your eyes, and think about the values that are most important to you. See the vision that you've put together and how future you will come into being. Really feel this future in your body as if it's already here and you've achieved that vision.

Now open your eyes and know that you will never be stuck again.

ACKNOWLEDGMENTS

AS I WROTE in chapter 9, during a week in the fall of 2020, I met with three male tech CEOs who were all writing books. After those discussions, I reflected on the cycle of influence and success in business. Leaders who publish books are invited to present on stages and give commentary in media outlets. They are quoted in boardrooms and classrooms, win awards, and grow their businesses and careers. After the success of the first round, some write more books, and the cycle starts again. All that success made me wonder how many women are writing business books. I found the answer in the *New York Times* on the 2022 business book bestsellers list— only 15 percent of the authors were women that year. Right then I had a vision to get more women writing and publishing business books. Over the next weeks, I talked about this vision constantly with my best friend, my husband, Mike, and continued to figure out how I could encourage more women leaders to write books. "You're going to have to write a book if you want to encourage other women to write books, too," he said. "Well, I don't know even know how to write a book!" I yelled back. "You can figure it out" was his comeback. Using that encouragement and knowing that I had found the problem I wanted to run headfirst into, the idea for The 10 was created. The 10 would be a group of incredible women business leaders coming together to write our first books and help each other figure it out. The first woman to partner with me in this goal was Lindsay Riddell, followed by Thomasina Williams, Dawn Crew, Sonya Pelia, Chelsea C. Williams, Kim Sample, Pushpinder Lubana, Lata Setty, Kelli Williams, Jeanette Jordan, and Tricia Timm, who was the first to be published with her award-winning book *Embrace the Power of You*. Thank you to Siena Brown, who supported our early work and believed in every one of us. And thank you to all the experts and authors who met with The 10 while we were writing our books. You showed us it could be done and that there was nothing to stop us from doing it.

At work and in life, I've had many mentors and supporters who have helped me navigate roles, career decisions, country moves, global issues, and thinking bigger. Aziz Hurzook and Bobby John, who hired me for my first job in tech, almost fired me, and they showed me what it takes to be in the top 10 percent. Roohi Saeed, who heard my ambition to work in the US and helped make it possible. Tracey Stout, who made the decision that changed my career trajectory. Steven Hoffman started out as a consultant I worked with but became the best challenger, thought partner, and friend. You always ask me the hard question at the right time. All the teams and clients I've worked with at Eastwick, Hotwire Global, and Enero who are as excited about the tech and innovation industry as I am and believe there is always more to accomplish. Thank you, Brent Scrimshaw, for giving me an opportunity to lead the global business at Hotwire, and Fiona Chilcott, for championing me.

Barbara Bates, who brought me into her business, included me in everything, and supported all my ambitions. Most importantly, she continues to show me how to celebrate everything and create a great life.

Thank you to the Page Two publishing team, who led me through the process of turning a half-done manuscript into the book you hold today. In discussions with co-founder Trena White, we found a powerful values alignment early on. Louise Hill, my project manager, brought together the team of Sarah Brohman, my editor who patiently worked through each round; designer Jennifer Lum, who developed the book cover options of my dreams; and my copy editor, Melissa Kawaguchi, who made sure each word is perfect.

So many friends and family who continued to be excited for the book, even when I was doubting the process: Ruth and Harold Kenney, Barbara Bates, Erin McCabe, Lisa Newton, Sherri Savoie, Julie and Greg Hingsbergen, Emily Haldeman, Debbie Younkin, and Bill Wohl. Jolawn Victor and Jesse Hamlin, thank you for helping me sort through cover options and picking the boldest one. Thank you, Aaryan Vira, for helping me with research and always checking in on how the big project was going.

My first supporter was my mom, Dorothy Blaikie. She told me every day that I could be anything I wanted to be, and I grew up believing it. Thank you to my biggest and best supporter who is wildly clapping and cheering for me in heaven.

My sister Megan, who always tells me exactly what she's thinking, even when I don't want to hear it. LG, Hannah, Leo, and Gavin, who remind me life is not all about work and should be mostly about playing games, eating candy, and being silly.

My kids, Madison and Cameron, brought me love, hugs, kisses, coffee, encouragement, and opinions throughout the creation of this book. I love them so much. I am so motivated to make them proud and show them they can be anything they want to be.

And Mike, who is my everything and always will be.

NOTES

Chapter 1: Stuck

Seventy percent of people: LearningNews, "75% Feel 'Stuck' Personally and Professionally," October 27, 2021, learningnews.com/news /learning-news/2021/75-stuck-personally-and-professionally/.

This activates your sympathetic nervous: "Understanding the Stress Response," Harvard Health Publishing, July 6, 2020, health.harvard .edu/staying-healthy/understanding-the-stress-response/.

Anxiety and depression in Black Americans: "Employee Mental Health & Well-Being During & Beyond COVID-19," American Psychiatric Association Center for Workplace Mental Health, workplacementalhealth.org/employer-resources/guides-and-toolkits/ employee-mental-health-well-being-during-beyond-co.

Did you know that only 9 percent: Marcel Shwantes, "Studies Show 91 Percent of Us Won't Achieve Our New Year's Resolutions," *Inc.*, January 8, 2022, inc.com/marcel-schwantes/ studies-show-91-percent-of-us-wont-achieve-our-new-years- resolutions-how-to-be-9-percent-that-do.html.

Chapter 2: Understanding Where You Want to Be

"I believed that all software": Marc Benioff and Carlye Adler, *Behind the Cloud: The Untold Story of How Salesforce.com Went from Idea to Billion-Dollar Company—and Revolutionized an Industry*, Jossey-Bass (2009).

"In this form, envy signals": Manfred F.R. Kets de Vries, "Turning Envy into a Positive Force," INSEAD, June 29, 2015, knowledge.insead.edu/leadership-organisations/turning-envy-positive-force.

"If you study science and history": Tim Ferriss, "Legendary Investor Bill Gurley on Investing Rules, Finding Outliers, Insights from Jeff Bezos and Howard Marks, Must-Read Books, Creating True Competitive Advantages, Open-Source Strategies, Adapting Mental Models to New Realities, and More (#651)," *The Tim Ferriss Show* (podcast), January 25, 2023, tim.blog/2023/01/25/bill-gurley/.

Podcast Index reports more than: Podcast Index, podcastindex.org/.

One of the examples he gives is about meeting a seminar leader: Jack Canfield and Janet Switzer, "Chapter 12," *The Success Principles*, HarperCollins (2015).

"The Law of Attraction simply states that like attracts like": Canfield, *The Success Principles*.

"Growth and comfort do not": Megan Barnett, "IBM's Ginni Rometty: Growth and Comfort Do Not Coexist," *Fortune*, October 5, 2011, fortune.com/2011/10/05/ibms-ginni-rometty-growth-and-comfort-do-not-coexist/.

Chapter 3: New Thinking

"a relatively uncontrolled cognitive": American Psychological Association, "Associative Thinking," APA Dictionary of Psychology, dictionary.apa.org/associative-thinking.

This model was introduced: Steve Coley, "Enduring Ideas: The Three Horizons of Growth," *McKinsey Quarterly*, December 1, 2009, mckinsey.com/capabilities/strategy-and-corporate-finance/our-insights/enduring-ideas-the-three-horizons-of-growth.

Chapter 4: Short-Term Tentative Goals

Canva's mission: Afdhel Aziz, "How Canva Is Being a Force for Good by Empowering the Whole World to Design," *Forbes*, March 31, 2022, forbes.com/sites/afdhelaziz/2022/03/31/how-canva-is-being-a-force-for-good-by-empowering-the-whole-world-to-design/.

"The purpose of life is to pursue happiness": Tom Huddleston Jr., "Zoom's Founder Left a 6-figure Job because He Wasn't Happy—and Following His Heart Made Him a Billionaire," Make It, August 21, 2019, cnbc.com/2019/08/21/zoom-founder-left-job-because-he-wasnt-happy-became-billionaire.html.

"If you're going to start a company around": Tim Ferriss, "The Tim Ferriss Show Transcripts: Marc Andreessen (#163)," *The Tim Ferriss Show,* January 1, 2018, tim.blog/2018/01/01/the-tim-ferriss-show -transcripts-marc-andreessen/.

He wrote a book called Subscribed: "About Zuora, Inc.," zuora.com/about/.

Chapter 5: Think and Act Big

In February 2021: Avery Hartmans and Annabelle Williams, "How Bumble Grew from a Female-Focused Dating App to a Global Behemoth Valued at Over $8 Billion after Going Public," *Insider,* February 11, 2021, businessinsider.com/ bumble-dating-app-company-history-2021-ipo-2020-9.

Its report revealed: Hard Numbers, "Exploring the Link between Thought Leadership on Social Media and Company Valuations," hardnumbers .co.uk/research-unicorn-edition.

Chapter 6: Unusual Moves

"The result is profitable": Ben Lutkevich, "Coopetition (co-opetition)," TechTarget, September 2021, techtarget.com/searchcio/definition/ co-opetition.

"What it unlocked was actually a totally": Brianne Garrett, "Why Collaborating with Your Competition Can Be a Great Idea," *Forbes,* September 19, 2019, forbes.com/sites/briannegarrett/2019/09/19/ why-collaborating-with-your-competition-can-be-a-great-idea/.

Coined "the Say Gap": "The PR Council and its Member Firms Launch Close the Say Gap, Aim to Make Women's Expertise More Visible," PR Council, March 4, 2020, prcouncil.net/news/ the-pr-council-and-its-member-firms-launch-close-the-say-gap-aim-to-make-womens-expertise-more-visible/.

It's not hard to figure: Nathaniel Meyersohn, "Stores Live in Fear of Amazon. The Kohl's CEO Embraced It," CNN Business, March 11, 2019, cnn.com/2019/03/10/business/kohls-ceo-michelle-gass-profile/index.html.

As an industry-wide team: David Shepardson, "Google, Ford, Uber Launch Coalition to Further Self-Driving Cars," Reuters, April 26, 2016, reuters.com/article/us-autos-selfdriving-idUSKCNOXN1F1.

"Focused on the insights of": Expert Panel, "15 Tech Industry Leaders Share Best Practices for Effective Beta Testing," *Forbes*, May 25, 2021, forbes.com/sites/forbestechcouncil/2021/05/25/15-tech-industry-leaders-share-best-practices-for-effective-beta-testing/.

A McKinsey article: Alessandro Buffoni, Alice de Angelis, Volker Grüntges, "How to Make Sure Your Next Product or Service Launch Drives Growth," McKinsey & Company, October 13, 2017, mckinsey.com/capabilities/growth-marketing-and-sales/our-insights/how-to-make-sure-your-next-product-or-service-launch-drives-growth.

Chapter 7: Creating New

"It was just an aha moment": Guy Raz, "HIBT Lab! Goodr: Jasmine Crowe-Houston," *How I Built This* (podcast), November 24, 2022, podcasts.apple.com/us/podcast/hibt-lab-goodr-jasmine-crowe-houston/id1150510297?i=1000586511843.

At the time of the writing this book, Crunchbase: "Goodr," Crunchbase, crunchbase.com/organization/goodr/company_financials.

"Are we going to fold, or are we going to fight?": Shellye Archambeau, *Unapologetically Ambitious: Take Risks, Break Barriers, and Create Success on Your Own Terms*, Grand Central Publishing (2020), 181.

"We acted on our rallying cry": Archambeau, *Unapologetically Ambitious*, 190.

Kalanick's strategy was simple: Mike Isaac, *Super Pumped: The Battle for Uber*, W.W. Norton (2019).

"Over time, this pivoting may": Eric Reiss, "Pivot, Don't Jump to a New Vision," *Startup Lessons Learned*, June 22, 2009, startuplessonslearned.com/2009/06/pivot-dont-jump-to-new-vision.html.

By August 2013, the company: Kate Clark, "The Slack Origin Story,"
   TechCrunch, May 30, 2019, techcrunch.com/2019/05/30/
   the-slack-origin-story/.

Marc Benioff, CEO of Salesforce: Catherine Clifford, "Salesforce CEO
   Marc Benioff: Why We Have 'Mindfulness Zones' Where Employees
   Put Away Phones, Clear Their Minds," Make It, November 5, 2019,
   cnbc.com/2019/11/05/salesforce-ceo-marc-benioff-why-we-have-
   mindfulness-zones.html.

"Sixty-two per cent of Gen Z": Alice Jeffery, "How Millennials
   and Gen Z Turned Astrology into a Billion-Dollar Industry,"
   Harper's Bazaar, January 2023, harpersbazaar.com.au/
   why-are-people-obsessed-with-astrology/.

"part of the positive stress movement": Christina Farr, "Tech Elites Are
   Fasting and Taking Ice Baths to Push Their Bodies to Work Harder,"
   CNBC, March 1, 2018, cnbc.com/2018/03/01/tech-elites-embracing-
   positive-stress-cold-showers-extreme-diets.html.

Chapter 8: Keep Going

"Two years later, I acquired": Jerome Knyszewski, "Jaclyn Baumgarten
   of Boatsetter; How to Tale Your Company from Good to
   Great," *Authority Magazine*, medium.com/authority-magazine/
   jaclyn-baumgarten-of-boatsetter-how-to-take-your-company-from-
   good-to-great-9dd636c7edbd.

Self-sabotage keeps you stuck: Evelyn Marinoff, "Why We
   Self-sabotage (and 3 Ways to Stop Doing It)," *Fast
   Company*, July 7, 2020, fastcompany.com/90524642/
   why-we-self-sabotage-and-3-ways-to-stop-doing-it.

"When we compared our research participants": Teresa M. Amabile and
   Steven J. Kramer, "The Power of Small Wins," *Harvard Business
   Review*, May 2011, hbr.org/2011/05/the-power-of-small-wins.

"Open source is way": Tim Ferriss, "Legendary Investor Bill Gurley on
   Investing Rules, Finding Outlines, Insights from Jeff Bezos and
   Howard Marks, Must-Read Books, Creating True Competitive
   Advantages, Open-Source Strategies, Adapting Mental Models to
   New Realities, and More," *The Tim Ferriss Show*, January 25, 2023,
   tim.blog/2023/01/25/bill-gurley/.

SOURCES

Books

Archambeau, Shellye. *Unapologetically Ambitious: Take Risks, Break Barriers, and Create Success on Your Own Terms.* Grand Central Publishing, 2022.

Benioff, Marc. *Behind the Cloud: The Untold Story of How Salesforce.com Went from Idea to Billion-Dollar Company—and Revolutionized an Industry.* Wiley, 2009.

Canfield, Jack, with Janet Switzer. *The Success Principles: How to Get from Where You Are to Where You Want to Be.* HarperElement, 2005.

Clark, Dorie. *Entrepreneurial You: Monetize Your Expertise, Create Multiple Income Streams, and Thrive.* Harvard Business Review Press, 2017.

Comstock, Beth, and Tahl Raz. *Imagine It Forward: Courage, Creativity, and the Power of Change.* Penguin Random House, 2018.

Doerr, John. *Measure What Matters: How Google, Bono, and the Gates Foundation Rock the World.* Portfolio, 2018.

Horowitz, Ben. *The Hard Thing about Hard Things: Building a Business When There Are No Easy Answers.* Harper Business, 2014.

Isaac, Mike. *Super Pumped: The Battle for Uber.* W. W. Norton, 2020.

Montalvo Timm, Tricia. *Embrace the Power of You: Owning Your Identity at Work.* Page Two, 2023.

Ries, Eric. *The Lean Startup: How Today's Entrepreneurs Use Continuous Innovation to Create Radically Successful Businesses.* Crown Business, 2011.

Rometty, Ginni. *Good Power: Leading Positive Change in Our Lives, Work, and World.* Harvard Business Review Press, 2023.

Saint John, Bozoma. *The Urgent Life: My Story of Love, Loss, and Survival.* Viking, 2023.

Podcasts

Corinne Crabtree. *Losing 100 Pounds with Corinne.*

Guy Raz. *How I Built This.*

Guy Raz. *Wisdom from the Top.*

Websites

Catalytic Thinking Labs: catalyticthinkinglabs.com/.

CNBC Make It: cnbc.com/make-it.

"Design Thinking Resources." IDEO: ideou.com/pages/design-thinking -resources.

"Systemic Inventive Thinking." Wikipedia: en.wikipedia.org/wiki/ Systematic_inventive_thinking.

Mental Health Resources

MentalHealth.gov provides one-stop access to US government mental health and mental health problems information: mentalhealth.gov/.

FindTreatment.gov is a confidential and anonymous resource for persons seeking treatment for mental and substance use disorders in the US and its territories: findtreatment.gov/.

988 Suicide & Crisis Lifeline provides free and confidential support 24/7 for people in distress, prevention and crisis resources for you or your loved ones, and best practices for professionals in the US: 988lifeline .org. In the US, dial 988.

ABOUT THE AUTHOR

EATHER KERNAHAN is a global business leader who has been featured in *Fast Company*, *Fortune*, Thrive Global, *Biz Women*, and *Ad Week*. She currently serves as the Global CEO of Hotwire Global, an award-winning global tech communications and marketing consultancy that has worked with companies such as Meta, Adobe, eBay, Pinterest, LinkedIn, and Honeywell. She was named one of the *San Francisco Business Times* 100 Most Influential Women and North America Innovator of the Year by Provoke Media. She serves on the board of ICCO, is a trustee of IPR, and is past board chair of the PR Council.

Kernahan is a sought-after speaker on business leadership topics and has taken the stage at Fortune Global Forum discussing innovation on the fast track, at the NASDAQ Entrepreneurial Center as a keynote speaker and workshop facilitator on unlocking authentic leadership, and at Chief discussing high stakes leadership. She is a strategic adviser and has been a mentor to leaders, entrepreneurs, and start-ups through work with NASDAQ Entrepreneurial Center,

Company Ventures—NYC's foremost venture community—Scotians Global Advisors, Cleantech Open, Women's Startup Lab, and the LAGRANT Foundation. She is a venture capitalist and LP with Women Who Invest and Portfolia.

Taking action in the areas of inclusion, belonging, and education is important to her. She has been part of the launch team of the Say Gap, a program developed by the PR Council to train women and other underrepresented leaders to speak on stage and be interviewed by the press. She co-founded The 10, a group of women in leadership who are working to have more women leaders write and publish their first business books. As well, she serves on the Citizen's Bond Oversight Committee for the College of Marin.

Her career in technology started in Toronto, Canada, and she has since held senior marketing and leadership roles at start-up, midsize, and global tech companies in Canada and the US, where she has been part of teams building the future. She received her master's in business administration in sustainable enterprise from Dominican University of California, bachelor of arts from Saint Mary's University in Halifax, Nova Scotia, and certificate in public relations from the Nova Scotia Community College. She lives in the San Francisco Bay area with her husband and children.

AUTHOR MARKETING SERVICES

If you've done the work through this book and you're now unstuck, please share the ideas that worked best for you with others in your community. As you've learned, open source is a powerful model for lifting everyone up.

Gift this book to your team, network, mentors, family, and friends.

Bring it to your book club and use the book club resources from Unstuckable.me to guide you.

There isn't a person on this planet who hasn't felt stuck at some point and needed support and tools to move forward. You are now fully prepared to help them learn to be unstuck, just like you are.

Good luck and please connect with me to share your unstuckable successes:

- Unstuckable.me
- @hkernahan
- linkedin.com/in/heatherkernahan/
- @hkernahan